Outlook 2013:
Basic
Student Manual

MOS Edition

Outlook 2013: Basic

Chief Executive Officer, Axzo Press:	Ken Wasnock
Series Designer and COO:	Adam A. Wilcox
Vice President, Operations:	Josh Pincus
Director of Publishing Systems Development:	Dan Quackenbush
Writer:	Audrey Stevenson
Keytester:	Cliff Coryea

Trademarks

ILT Series is a trademark of Axzo Press.

Some of the product names and company names used in this book have been used for identification purposes only and may be trademarks or registered trademarks of their respective manufacturers and sellers.

Disclaimer

We reserve the right to revise this publication and make changes from time to time in its content without notice.

ISBN 10: 1-4260-3628-0
ISBN 13: 978-1-4260-3628-6

Printed in the United States of America

1 2 3 4 5 GL 06 05 04 03

Contents

Introduction

After reading this introduction, you will know how to:

A Use ILT Series manuals in general.

B Use prerequisites, a target student description, course objectives, and a skills inventory to properly set your expectations for the course.

C Re-key this course after class.

Topic A: About the manual

ILT Series philosophy

Our manuals facilitate your learning by providing structured interaction with the software itself. While we provide text to explain difficult concepts, the hands-on activities are the focus of our courses. By paying close attention as your instructor leads you through these activities, you will learn the skills and concepts effectively.

We believe strongly in the instructor-led class. During class, focus on your instructor. Our manuals are designed and written to facilitate your interaction with your instructor, and not to call attention to manuals themselves.

We believe in the basic approach of setting expectations, delivering instruction, and providing summary and review afterwards. For this reason, lessons begin with objectives and end with summaries. We also provide overall course objectives and a course summary to provide both an introduction to and closure on the entire course.

Manual components

The manuals contain these major components:

- Table of contents
- Introduction
- Units
- Course summary
- Glossary
- Index

Each element is described below.

Table of contents

The table of contents acts as a learning roadmap.

Introduction

The introduction contains information about our training philosophy and our manual components, features, and conventions. It contains target student, prerequisite, objective, and setup information for the specific course.

Units

Units are the largest structural component of the course content. A unit begins with a title page that lists objectives for each major subdivision, or topic, within the unit. Within each topic, conceptual and explanatory information alternates with hands-on activities. Units conclude with a summary comprising one paragraph for each topic, and an independent practice activity that gives you an opportunity to practice the skills you've learned.

The conceptual information takes the form of text paragraphs, exhibits, lists, and tables. The activities are structured in two columns, one telling you what to do, the other providing explanations, descriptions, and graphics.

Course summary

This section provides a text summary of the entire course. It is useful for providing closure at the end of the course. The course summary also indicates the next course in this series, if there is one, and lists additional resources you might find useful as you continue to learn about the software.

Glossary

The glossary provides definitions for all of the key terms used in this course.

Index

The index at the end of this manual makes it easy for you to find information about a particular software component, feature, or concept.

Manual conventions

We've tried to keep the number of elements and the types of formatting to a minimum in the manuals. This aids in clarity and makes the manuals more classically elegant looking. But there are some conventions and icons you should know about.

Item	Description
Italic text	In conceptual text, indicates a new term or feature.
Bold text	In unit summaries, indicates a key term or concept. In an independent practice activity, indicates an explicit item that you select, choose, or type.
`Code font`	Indicates code or syntax.
`Longer strings of ▶ code will look ▶ like this.`	In the hands-on activities, any code that's too long to fit on a single line is divided into segments by one or more continuation characters (▶). This code should be entered as a continuous string of text.
Select **bold item**	In the left column of hands-on activities, bold sans-serif text indicates an explicit item that you select, choose, or type.
Keycaps like (↵ ENTER)	Indicate a key on the keyboard you must press.

Hands-on activities

The hands-on activities are the most important parts of our manuals. They are divided into two primary columns. The "Here's how" column gives short instructions to you about what to do. The "Here's why" column provides explanations, graphics, and clarifications. Here's a sample:

Do it!   ## A-1:   Creating a commission formula

Here's how	Here's why
1 Open Sales	This is an oversimplified sales compensation worksheet. It shows sales totals, commissions, and incentives for five sales reps.
2 Observe the contents of cell F4	F4 ▼ ▪ = =E4*C_Rate
	The commission rate formulas use the name "C_Rate" instead of a value for the commission rate.

For these activities, we have provided a collection of data files designed to help you learn each skill in a real-world business context. As you work through the activities, you will modify and update these files. Of course, you might make a mistake and therefore want to re-key the activity starting from scratch. To make it easy to start over, you will rename each data file at the end of the first activity in which the file is modified. Our convention for renaming files is to add the word "My" to the beginning of the file name. In the above activity, for example, a file called "Sales" is being used for the first time. At the end of this activity, you would save the file as "My sales," thus leaving the "Sales" file unchanged. If you make a mistake, you can start over using the original "Sales" file.

In some activities, however, it might not be practical to rename the data file. If you want to retry one of these activities, ask your instructor for a fresh copy of the original data file.

Topic B: Setting your expectations

Properly setting your expectations is essential to your success. This topic will help you do that by providing:

- Prerequisites for this course
- A description of the target student
- A list of the objectives for the course
- A skills assessment for the course

Course prerequisites

Before taking this course, you should be familiar with personal computers and the use of a keyboard and a mouse. Furthermore, this course assumes that you've completed the following courses or have equivalent experience:

- *Windows XP: Basic, Windows Vista: Basic,* or *Windows 7: Basic*

Target student

The target student for the course is an individual who wants to learn the basic features of Outlook 2013 and use them to create and manage e-mail messages, contacts, appointments, meetings, and tasks.

Course objectives

These overall course objectives will give you an idea about what to expect from the course. It is also possible that they will help you see that this course is not the right one for you. If you think you either lack the prerequisite knowledge or already know most of the subject matter to be covered, you should let your instructor know that you think you are misplaced in the class.

After completing this course, you will know how to:

- Identify elements of the Outlook environment; use and customize Outlook Today
- Read, create, and send e-mail messages; reply to, format, and check spelling in messages; forward, delete, and restore messages; work with attachments; and print messages
- Set delivery options for messages; flag messages; request a read receipt; use and create views for your mail; arrange, sort, and filter messages; use Instant Search to quickly search the current folder; and specify settings for controlling junk e-mail.
- Use Contacts to add, modify, and organize business and personal contacts; use different views to show contact details; customize an electronic business card; manage and use address books; and create contact groups.
- Use the Tasks folder to add, edit, and mark tasks; assign tasks; accept or decline a task request; send an update; and track an assigned task.
- Use the Calendar to create single and recurring appointments; change and delete appointments; add events and holidays to the Calendar; and change views.
- Use the Calendar to schedule meetings; read and respond to meeting requests; reserve resources; manage meeting responses; and update and cancel meetings.

Skills inventory

Use the following form to gauge your skill level entering the class. For each skill listed, rate your familiarity from 1 to 5, with five being the most familiar. *This is not a test.* Rather, it is intended to provide you with an idea of where you're starting from at the beginning of class. If you're wholly unfamiliar with all the skills, you might not be ready for the class. If you think you already understand all of the skills, you might need to move on to the next course in the series. In either case, you should let your instructor know as soon as possible.

Skill	1	2	3	4	5
Identifying elements of the Outlook window					
Using the Folder pane					
Using the Reading pane					
Accessing folders from Outlook Today					
Customizing Outlook Today					
Previewing and reading messages					
Creating, formatting, and sending messages					
Checking a message's spelling					
Replying to and forwarding messages					
Deleting and restoring messages					
Sending and forwarding attachments					
Compressing large image attachments					
Previewing and saving attachments					
Customizing the page setup for printing					
Printing messages and attachments					
Defining delivery options					
Flagging an email message					
Using delivery and read receipts					
Working with views					
Renaming and moving Inbox folders					
Arranging, sorting, searching, and filtering messages					
Adding senders to the Blocked Senders or Safe Senders lists					

Skill	1	2	3	4	5
Marking a message as not junk					
Changing options for managing junk email					
Adding and modifying contacts					
Attaching items to a contact					
Adding a contact from the same company as a previous contact					
Forwarding and saving contacts					
Editing an electronic business card					
Printing contacts					
Using address books					
Importing contacts					
Creating and using a contact group					
Updating a contact group					
Forwarding and deleting a contact group					
Adding contact group notes					
Creating and deleting tasks					
Editing tasks					
Adding recurring tasks					
Marking a task as completed					
Assigning tasks					
Accepting a task request					
Sending task status reports					
Tracking assigned tasks					
Printing tasks					
Setting up appointments					
Adding and modifying recurring appointments					
Deleting and restoring appointments					
Adding events					

Skill	1	2	3	4	5
Changing the work day times in the Calendar					
Displaying multiple time zones					
Adding holidays to the calendar					
Printing calendars					
Creating and sending meeting requests					
Adding and modifying recurring meetings					
Reading and accepting a meeting request					
Responding to a New Time Proposed message					
Declining a meeting request					
Updating a meeting					
Reserving resources in a meeting request					
Reviewing meeting responses					
Adding meeting attendees					
Canceling meetings					

Topic C: Re-keying the course

If you have the proper hardware and software, you can re-key this course after class. This section explains what you'll need in order to do so, and how to do it.

Hardware requirements

The Exchange server should have:

- A keyboard and a mouse
- At least 1 GHz 32-bit or 1.4 GHz 64-bit processor (2 GHz or faster recommended)
- At least 1 GB RAM (2 GB or greater recommended)
- At least 50 GB hard drive
- A DVD-ROM drive
- A monitor with at least 1024 × 768 resolution

The student computer should have:

- A keyboard and a mouse
- At least 1 GHz 32-bit or 64-bit processor
- At least 1 GB RAM
- At least 50 GB hard drive with at least 15 GB of available space
- A DVD-ROM drive
- A graphics card that supports DirectX 9 graphics with:
  - WDDM driver
  - 128 MB of graphics memory (minimum)
  - Pixel Shader 2.0 in hardware
  - 32 bits per pixel
- A monitor with at least 1024 × 768 resolution

Software requirements

You will need the following software:

- Windows Server 2008 Standard 64-bit Edition with Service Pack 2
- Windows 7 Professional
- Microsoft Exchange Server 2010 Standard Edition
- Microsoft Outlook 2013
- A printer driver (An actual printer is not required, but students will not be able to complete the "Printing messages and attachments" activity in Unit 2, the "Printing contacts" activity in Unit 4, and the "Printing a Calendar" activity in Unit 6 unless a driver is installed.)

Network requirements

The following network components and connectivity are also required for this course:

- Internet access, for the following purposes:
  - Downloading the latest critical updates and service packs from www.windowsupdate.com
  - Completing activities throughout the course

- A static IPv4 address on the same subnet as the computers. You will need a DHCP server available on that subnet and a pool of addresses sufficient for the all computers.
- A network printer.

Setup instructions to re-key the course

Before you re-key the course, you will need to perform the following steps.

Windows server 2008 installation

1 Install Windows Server 2008 Standard. When prompted, enter and confirm a password of **!pass1234** for the Administrator account.

2 Configure the server, using the Initial Configuration Tasks window.

    A Set the correct time zone and time.

    B Configure a static IPv4 address for the Local Area Connection. Disable IPv6.

    C Name the computer **winserver**. Restart when prompted.

    D Install the Active Directory Domain Services role. Create a new domain, **outlanderspices.com**, in a new forest.

3 Turn off Internet Explorer Enhanced Security Configuration.

4 Install Windows Server 2008 Service Pack 2.

Exchange Server 2010 installation

1 From the Exchange Server DVD, install the .NET Framework 3.5 SP1 components.

2 Install the Windows PowerShell v2.

3 Use Windows PowerShell to install the required server components by running this command:
```
ServerManagerCmd -ip d:\scripts\Exchange-Typical.xml
```

4 Use Windows PowerShell to start the NetTcpPortSharing service by running this command:
```
Set-Service NetTcpPortSharing -StartupType Automatic
```

5 Visit **http://go.microsoft.com/fwlink/?LinkID=191548** to download and install the 2010 Office System Converter: Microsoft Filter Pack.

6 From the Exchange Server DVD, install the Exchange Language option, installing only languages from the DVD.

7 Install Microsoft Exchange, following the Typical Exchange Server Installation options. Use **Outlander Spices** as the organization name.

8   From the Exchange Server setup program, install critical updates for Microsoft Exchange.

9   Click Start and choose All Programs. If you do not see a Microsoft Exchange Server 2010 menu option, then not all components were installed. Insert the Exchange DVD in your drive and run Setup.exe. When prompted, make sure that "Mailbox server," "Client Access server," and "Hub Transport server" are checked. Check the missing roles and proceed again through the installation wizard to install them.

Creating user accounts on the server

You will need to create two user accounts for yourself and one for the Instructor role. Name the accounts **Instructor**, **Student01**, and **Student02**.

Use Active Directory Users and Computers to create each account. Use **!pass1234** for the password. Uncheck "User must change password at next logon." Check "User cannot change password" and "Password never expires."

Creating mailboxes

Create a mailbox associated with each user account:

1   On the Exchange server, click Start and choose All Programs, Microsoft Exchange Server 2010, Exchange Management Console.

2   Expand Microsoft Exchange on-Premises (winserver.outlanderspices.com).

3   Select Recipient Configuration.

4   In the middle pane, right-click and choose New Mailbox.

5   With User Mailbox selected, click Next.

6   Select Existing users. Click Add.

7   Select all of the accounts you added (use Ctrl+click or Shift+click to select them all) and click OK. Click Next.

8   Click Next. Click New to create a mailbox for each user you selected.

9   Click Finish. Close the Exchange Management Console.

Creating mailboxes for resources

1   On the Exchange server, click Start and choose All Programs, Microsoft Exchange Server 2010, Exchange Management Console.

2   Expand Microsoft Exchange on-Premises (winserver.outlanderspices.com).

3   Select Recipient Configuration.

4   In the middle pane, right-click and choose New Mailbox.

5   Select Room Mailbox and then click Next.

6   Click Next.

7   Enter the following user account details and then click Next:

Name: **Conference Room A**

User logon name: **conf_room_A**

Password: **P@ssword**

8   In the Alias box, enter **CR_A** and then click Next.

9   Click Next, click New, and then click Finish to create the mailbox.

10 Close the Exchange Management Console.

Setting up the client computer or computers

You will need at least one client computer (you can log onto the same computer twice by using the Switch User option). For each client computer:

1   Install Windows 7 on an NTFS partition according to the software manufacturer's instructions. Name the computer **Computer01**, **Computer02**, or **Instructor**, depending on its role.

2   Configure each computer to use your classroom server as the DNS server.

3   On each computer, join the classroom domain.

4   Log onto the domain.

5   Install Microsoft Office 2013 according to the software manufacturer's instructions.

6   On each computer, configure Outlook to connect to the corresponding student account mailbox. For example, on Computer01, connect Outlook to the Student01 mailbox.

7   Connect to a network printer, installing drivers as necessary.

8   If you have the data disc that came with this manual, locate the Student Data folder on it and copy it to your Windows desktop.

   If you don't have the data disc, you can download the Student Data files for the course:

   a   Connect to http://downloads.logicaloperations.com.
   b   Enter the course title or search by part to locate this course
   c   Click the course title to display a list of available downloads.
       Note: Data Files are located under the Instructor Edition of the course.
   d   Click the link(s) for downloading the Student Data files.
   e   Create a folder named Student Data on the desktop of your computer.
   f   Double-click the downloaded zip file(s) and drag the contents into the Student Data folder.

9   From the instructor's computer, send two e-mail messages to each student. Make sure to send copies of the messages to the Instructor account as well. For the first message, use the subject "Welcome to Outlook 2013" and enter a message of your choice in the message area. For the second message, use "Your second message" as the subject and enter a message of your choice.

Unit 1

Getting started

Complete this unit, and you'll know how to:

A Identify the components of the Outlook environment, and use Outlook panes and folders.

B Use Outlook Today to keep track of your schedule and tasks for today, and customize the Outlook Today page.

Topic A: The program window

Explanation

Outlook is a Microsoft application that you can use to send and receive email. *Email* is an electronic message sent from one computer to another. You can also use Outlook as a personal organizer; for example, you can schedule meetings and appointments and keep track of tasks and contacts.

Any email message, contact, or task created in Outlook is called an *item*. Items are stored in folders, such as Inbox, Calendar, Contacts, and Tasks. These folders help you organize information. You can access the items within each folder by using the buttons in the Outlook window.

You can start Outlook by clicking Start and choosing All Programs, Microsoft Office 2013, Outlook 2013. The Outlook window is shown with elements that are common to other Windows-based applications—such as a title bar and a status bar—along with elements that are common to the Microsoft Office 2013 suite of applications. The Office-specific elements, shown in Exhibit 1-1, are the Quick Access toolbar and the Ribbon.

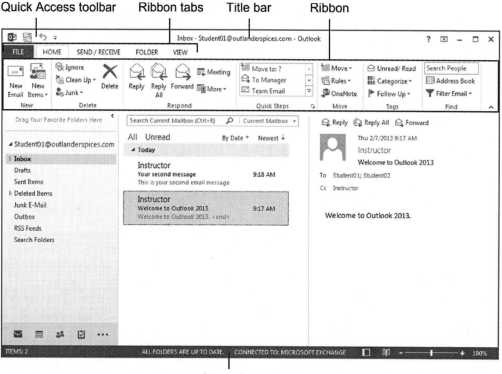

Exhibit 1-1: The Outlook window

The following table describes some of the elements shown in Exhibit 1-1.

Element	Description
Quick Access toolbar	Contains a customizable selection of commonly used buttons. By default, it contains the Send/Receive, Undo, and Customize Quick Access Toolbar buttons.
Ribbon	Contains tabs, each of which contains groups of related commands.
Title bar	Displays the name of the folder being displayed (in Exhibit 1-1, the Inbox of the Student01 user account) and the program name.
Status bar	Displays status information and contains buttons for commands that control the program's display (such as zooming in or out).

The Outlook window also contains elements that are specific to the Outlook application. These elements include a Folder pane with Navigation Bar, a Message List, and a Reading pane, as shown in Exhibit 1-2. The Folder pane shows the folders for each view, such as the Mail or Calendar views. The Message List displays the Folder Contents list. The Reading pane displays email messages.

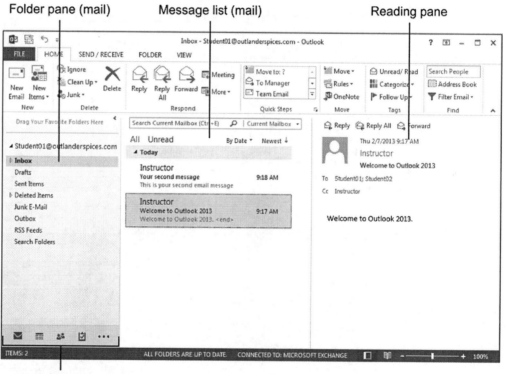

Exhibit 1-2: The Outlook window, with Outlook-specific elements labeled

The following table describes the common elements of the Outlook program window, shown in Exhibit 1-2.

Element	Description
Folder pane (formerly called Navigation pane)	Provides centralized navigation to all parts of Outlook. Displays the active pane, plus the Navigation bar at the bottom.
Navigation bar (formerly called Pane-switching buttons)	Display buttons for access to commonly used views (such as Mail, Calendar, and Contacts) with one click.
Message list	Displays the contents of the active mail folder.
Reading pane	Displays the contents of the selected email message.

Resizing a pane

You can increase or decrease the width of an individual pane in the program window. To do so, point to the border of the pane so that the pointer appears as a double-headed arrow, and then drag the border to the left or right.

Do it!

A-1:   Exploring the Outlook window

Here's how	Here's why
1 Click **Start** and choose **All Programs**, **Microsoft Office 2013**, **Outlook 2013**	To start Microsoft Outlook.
2 Observe the window	As shown in Exhibit 1-1 and Exhibit 1-2. The Outlook window contains various elements, such as the Title bar, the Ribbon, the Folder pane with Navigation bar, the Message list, and the Reading pane.
3 Observe the Ribbon	
	The Home tab is active. It contains commonly used commands for sending mail, organizing your messages, and managing your calendar.
Click the **Send/Receive** tab	To activate the tab and display commands related to sending and receiving messages.
Click the **Home** tab	To activate the tab.

4 Observe the Navigation pane

> Drag Your Favorite Folders Here ‹
>
> ⊿ Student01@outlanderspices.com
> **Inbox**
> Drafts
> Sent Items

By default, this pane shows your mail folders. At the top is a place where you can place a customizable list of frequently used folders. Below that list are folders associated with your email accounts. Below those folders are buttons, such as Calendar, Contacts, and Tasks, that you can click to display other panes and folders.

5 Observe the Message list

> Search Current Mailbox (Ctrl+E) 🔍 | Current Mailbox ▾
>
> All Unread   By Date ▾ Newest ↓
> ⊿ **Today**
>
> Instructor
> Your second message   9:18 AM
> This is your second email message

It displays messages stored in the folder that is selected in the Folder pane (Inbox, in this example). The Message list also contains a search box you can use to find items in the folder.

6 Observe the Reading pane

> ⤺ Reply ⤺ Reply All ⤻ Forward
>
> Thu 2/7/2013 9:18 AM
> Instructor
> **Your second message**
>
> To   Student01; Student02
> Cc   Instructor
>
> This is your second email message in Microsoft Outlook 2013.

It displays the contents of the message selected in the Message list.

7 Point to the right border of the Message list

> ↔|↔

The pointer changes to a double-headed arrow.

   Drag the border to the left

Press and hold the mouse button, and then move the mouse to decrease the width of the Message list.

The Folder pane and Navigation bar

The Folder pane and Navigation bar provide centralized navigation to all parts of Outlook. The Folder pane is found on the left side of the Outlook window and displays components of the current Outlook view, as shown in Exhibit 1-3. The Navigation bar allows you to navigate between Outlook views.

To switch the Navigation bar to Compact form, click the Navigation bar menu options button (icon with the three dots) and select Navigation Options. From the Navigation Options window, select Compact Navigation and click OK.

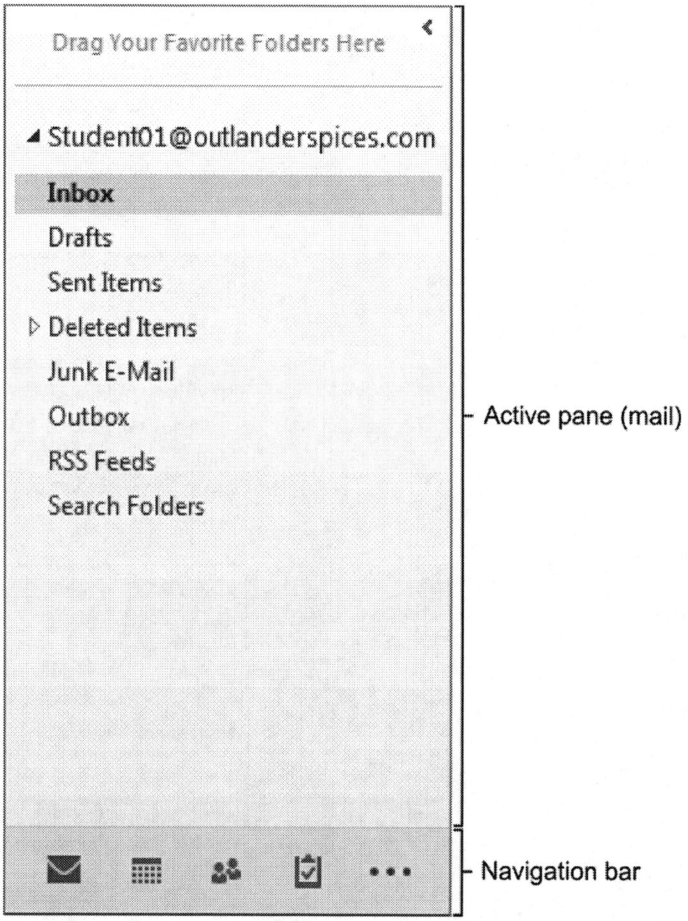

Drag Your Favorite Folders Here

▲ Student01@outlanderspices.com

Inbox

Drafts

Sent Items

▷ Deleted Items

Junk E-Mail

Outbox — Active pane (mail)

RSS Feeds

Search Folders

✉ ▦ 👥 ☑ • • • — Navigation bar

Exhibit 1-3: The Folder pane with the Mail pane active

Default views

Outlook provides several default views where you can access folders or shortcuts specific to each view. You can access a view by clicking the Navigation bar buttons in the Folder pane, shown in Exhibit 1-3. The following views are available by default: Mail, Calendar, People, and Tasks.

Menu options for the Notes, Folders, and Shortcuts views are available when you click the Ellipse button with the three dots that is located on the right side of the Navigation bar, along with the Navigation Options menu option.

The following table describes the built-in views that are housed in the Navigation bar.

Item	Description
Mail	Displays folders designated as Favorites, including your Inbox, Sent Items, and Deleted Items folders, as shown in Exhibit 1-3. Below that section, the pane displays all of your mail folders, including Drafts, Junk Email, and Search Folders.
Calendar	Displays the Date Navigator, which is a small calendar that displays the current month and the next month. Also, displays links to your My Calendars folder, which includes your calendar and possibly other users' calendars.
People	Displays the Contacts folder, plus a link to connect to a social network.
Tasks	Displays links to your To-Do List and Tasks folders.
Notes	Displays links to your Notes folders.
Folder List	Displays all of your folders, including Journal Folders.
Shortcuts	Contains links to Outlook Today and Microsoft Office Online.

Minimizing and expanding the Navigation pane

You can free up space in your Outlook window by minimizing the Folder pane. To minimize or expand the Navigation pane, either click the sideways-caret symbol (< or >) at the top corner of the pane, or click the View tab and choose Normal, Minimized, or Off from the Folder Pane menu. The minimized Folder pane, as shown in Exhibit 1-4, still provides access to the folders and files that you use most often.

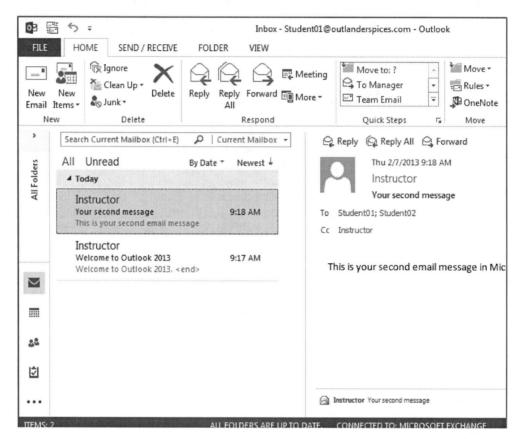

Exhibit 1-4: The Folder pane, on the left, is collapsed

Peeks

With Peeks, you can take a quick glance at your schedule, an appointment, people, or tasks without switching between views with the Navigation bar. When you place and pause your mouse pointer over the Calendar, People, or Tasks buttons on the Navigation bar, a peek window appears showing information about the view. For example, when you hover your mouse over the Calendar button, a calendar of the current month and today's scheduled items appears, as shown in Exhibit 1-5. You can click a date on the calendar to jump to a listing of appointments and meetings for another date.

If you would like for a peek to always be in view, you can dock it by clicking the Dock the peek button in the upper-right corner of the Peek window. This places the peek on the right side of the Outlook window, so it is always in view. If you are in the Mail view and dock the Calendar peek, it will only be visible from the Mail view, unless you also dock the Calendar peek on the other views.

To remove a peek from the Outlook window, click the Close button in the upper-right corner of the docked peek window. Removing a docked peek from one view does not remove it from the other views.

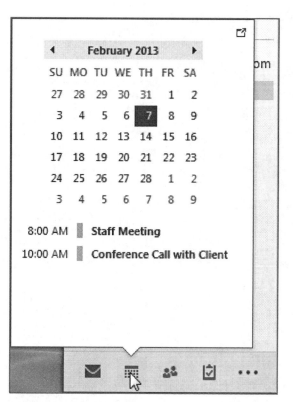

Exhibit 1-5: The Calendar peek

Do it!   ## A-2:   Examining the Folder pane

Here's how	Here's why
1 From the Navigation bar, click ✉	(If necessary.) To activate the Mail view. Notice that its contents are divided into Favorites and folders related to your email account.
2 From the Navigation bar, click ☑	To display the Tasks view and the contents of the Tasks folder, which is empty by default.
3 In the top-right corner of the Folder pane, click ‹	To minimize the Folder pane.
Click as shown ![All Folders]	To display the Task list in a flyout menu.
Expand the Folder pane	Click the sideways-caret icon (>) at the top of the pane.

4 Place the pointer over the Calendar button	In the Navigation bar. The Calendar peek with today's appointments is shown.
Click another date on the calendar	To see how you can take a quick glance of events scheduled for any date on the calendar.
Click ⬚	To dock the Calendar peek to the Tasks view.
Close the Calendar peek	(Click the X button.) To close the docked Calendar peek from the Tasks view.
5 Click ⬚	To show the Navigation bar menu options. Notice that options are available for Notes, Folders, Shortcuts, and Navigation Options.
6 Click **Notes**	A blank area appears to the right in the Outlook window.
7 Click **Folders**	(From the Navigation bar menu.) To display the default Outlook folders.
8 Click **Shortcuts**	(From the Navigation bar menu.) The shortcuts menu is empty by default, but you can add groups and shortcuts by right-clicking on the Shortcuts text.
9 Click **Navigation Options**	(From the Navigation bar menu.) To display the Navigation Options window. You can show additional views or change the order in which the buttons appear in the Navigation bar.
Check **Compact Navigation** and click OK	The Navigation bar now shows its categories as icons rather than words.

Outlook folders

Explanation   Outlook provides folders in which you can save and store the items you create. You can access these folders by using the default views within the Folders pane. You can also access a folder by clicking Folders from the Navigation bar menu and then clicking the folder you want. You can use the default folders or create your own folders.

By default, only the most relevant folders for any given view are displayed. For example, when the Mail view is active, your Inbox, Drafts, Sent Items, and other folders are visible, but the Calendar folder is not. Two folder list views are shown in Exhibit 1-6.

```
◢ Student01@outlanderspices.com        ◢ Student01@outlanderspices.com
  Inbox                                   Inbox
  Drafts                                  Drafts
  Sent Items                              Sent Items
  ▷ Deleted Items                        ▷ Deleted Items
  Junk E-Mail                             Calendar
  Outbox                                  Contacts
  RSS Feeds                               Journal
  Search Folders                          Junk E-Mail
                                          Notes
                                          Outbox
                                          RSS Feeds
                                        ▷ Sync Issues
                                          Tasks
                                          Search Folders
```

Exhibit 1-6: Two views of the Outlook folder list

The following table describes the default folders.

Folder	Description
<account address>	Click your email address to display the Outlook Today page, which provides a snapshot view of your activities planned for the day.
Inbox	You can create, send, receive, delete, and move messages from the Inbox.
Drafts	Stores unfinished items.
Sent Items	Stores copies of items you have sent to other people.
Deleted Items	Stores items that have been deleted from folders.
Calendar	Used to plan and schedule work-related and personal activities, such as appointments, meetings, and events.
Contacts	Stores information about people with whom you frequently communicate.
Journal	Can be used to keep a record of any interaction you want to remember. Stores actions that you choose relating to your contacts and places the actions in a timeline view.
Junk E-mail	Stores messages that were caught by the Junk Email filter.
Notes	Provides a place where you can keep reminders about important activities to complete and meetings to attend.
Outbox	Stores items created offline that you want to send the next time you are online.
RSS Feeds	Stores RSS (Really Simple Syndication) subscriptions so you can view data feeds from various news sources and Web logs (blogs).
Tasks	Used to list and manage the various activities you need to perform.
Search Folders	Displays the results of previously defined search queries.

Do it!

A-3: Accessing folders

Here's how	Here's why
1 Click ✉	To activate the Mail view and display the Inbox folder.
Compare the folder list for your email account to the left-hand graphic in Exhibit 1-6	The mail-related folders are listed first, followed by a selection of key folders related to communications activities.
2 Click •••	(On the right side of the Navigation bar.) To show the Navigation bar menu options.
Select **Folders**	The Favorites folder is hidden and your account's folder list is expanded to show the full list of folders.
3 In the folder list, click **Drafts**	To view the contents of your Drafts folder. It should be empty. This folder stores email messages you've started but not yet sent.
4 Click **Junk Email**	To view the contents of your Junk Email folder, which would contain messages that Outlook has determined are probably unsolicited commercial email (called "spam").
5 Click ✉	To restore the default view of Favorites and account-related folders. Doing so does not select the Inbox folder.
6 Click **Inbox**	To view your Inbox folder.

Context-sensitive tabs

Explanation   The commands available on the various tabs on the Ribbon depend on the folders and views you select. For example, the Home tab contains mail-related commands, as shown in Exhibit 1-7, when the Mail pane is active. But the Home tab shows calendar- and appointment-related commands, as shown in Exhibit 1-8, when the Calendar pane is active.

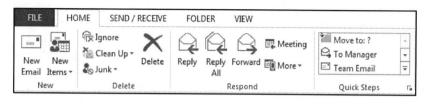

Exhibit 1-7: The Mail view's Home tab

Exhibit 1-8: The Calendar view's Home tab

Do it!

A-4:   Navigating tabs

Here's how	Here's why
1 Observe the Home tab	It contains commands for common email-related actions, such as sending or replying to messages.
2 Click the **Send/Receive** tab	To view its contents. This tab contains commands for processing email.
Click the **Folder** tab	Use commands on this tab to organize your email messages.
3 From the Navigation bar, click **Calendar**	To switch panes. The Calendar view's Home tab is active. It contains calendar-related commands.
4 Click the **Send/Receive** tab	To view its contents. Now this tab contains commands for processing calendar entries.
Click the **Folder** tab	The Calendar view's Folder tab is noticeably different from the Mail view's Folder tab.
5 From the Navigation bar, click **Mail**	To display the Mail view and its Home tab.

The Reading pane

Explanation

The Reading pane is displayed only when a mail-related view or folder is active. When the Mail view is active, the Reading pane appears to the right of the Message list, as shown in Exhibit 1-9. In the Reading pane, you can read the contents of an item, preview and open attachments, follow hyperlinks, use voting buttons, and respond to meeting requests.

If the Reading pane is not displayed, click the View tab, click the Reading Pane button, and choose an option from the menu that appears. Options include Right (default position), Bottom (below the Message list), and Off (hidden). If the Reading pane is Off, you can double-click a message to open it in its own window.

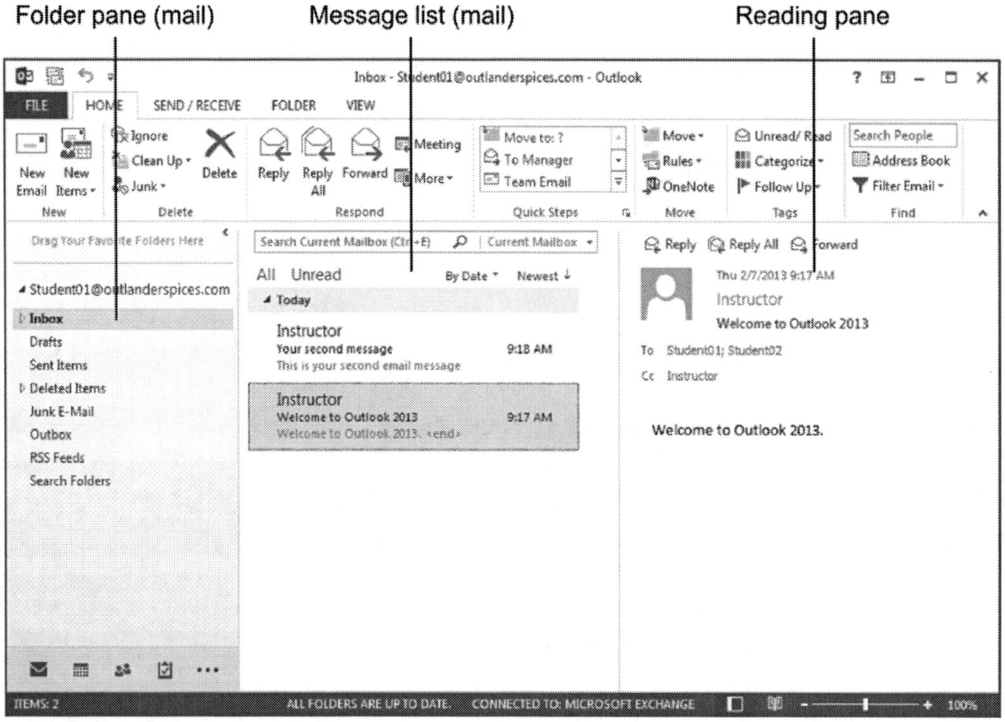

Folder pane (mail)   Message list (mail)   Reading pane

Exhibit 1-9: The location of the Reading pane

Do it!   **A-5:   Using the Reading pane**

Here's how	Here's why
1 Click as shown	All Unread By Date ▾ Newest ↓ ◢ Today Instructor Your second message 9:18 AM This is your second email message Instructor ▷ Welcome to Outlook 2013 ⬡ 9:17 AM ✕ Welcome to Outlook 2013. <end> (The message is in the Folder Contents list.) To select the message with the subject "Welcome to Outlook 2013" from the Instructor.
Observe the Reading pane	A preview of the message content automatically appears in the Reading pane.
2 Click the **View** tab	
In the Layout group, click **Reading Pane** and choose **Bottom**	▦ Folder Pane ▾ ▤ Reading Pane ▾ ▥ Right ▤ Bottom ▤ Off Options... The Reading pane appears at the bottom of your window.
3 Click **Reading Pane** and choose **Off**	To close the Reading pane.
Click **Reading Pane** and choose **Right**	To show the Reading pane in its default position.
4 In the Mail view, click **Sent Items**	To display the contents of the Sent Items folder. The folder is empty, and the Reading pane is blank.

Topic B: Outlook Today

Explanation

Outlook Today is another way to view a summary of your activities scheduled for the day. The summary displays your events, appointments, meetings, and tasks for the day. To display the Outlook Today view, click your account name (email address) in the Folder pane.

The Outlook Today page

The Outlook Today page is displayed in the space normally filled by the Message list and Reading panes. It contains three sections—Calendar, Tasks, and Messages—as shown in Exhibit 1-10. Summaries of your activities appear under the respective headings.

By default, under Calendar, you can see scheduled appointments for up to five days. Under Tasks, you'll see a summary of all task items you've created. Under Messages, you'll see the number of unread messages you have (in Inbox), the number of messages you've created but not sent (in Drafts), and the number of sent messages that have not left the computer (in Outbox). You can also click these headings to access the associated folders.

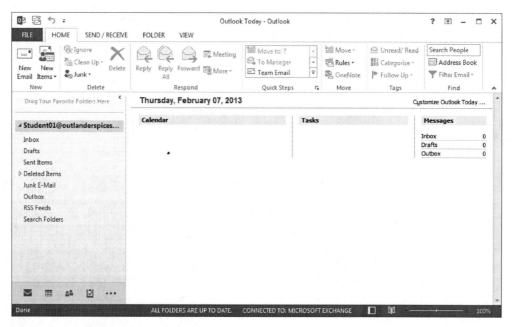

Exhibit 1-10: The Outlook Today page

Do it!

B-1: Accessing folders from Outlook Today

Here's how	Here's why
1 Click **Mail**	(If necessary.) In the Folder pane.
2 Select **Student##@outlanderspices.com**	(Where ## is your student number.) To display the Outlook Today page. It provides a summary of the day's plan.
3 Point to **Messages**	
	The pointer's shape changes to a hand, and the text is underlined.
Click **Messages**	To open the Mail view and the Inbox folder.

Customizing Outlook Today

Explanation

You can customize Outlook Today by using the Customize Outlook Today link, which is in the upper-right corner of the Outlook Today page. The following table describes some of the ways in which you can customize Outlook Today.

Option	Description
Startup	Displays the Outlook Today page when Outlook is opened.
Messages	Displays selected folders in the Messages section.
Calendar	Displays a specified number of days from your calendar in the Calendar section.
Tasks	Displays and sorts the selected tasks in the Tasks section.
Styles	Changes the layout or color scheme of the Outlook Today page.

Make your changes to customize Outlook Today, and then click Save Changes. Your customized settings will take effect immediately.

Do it!

B-2:   Customizing Outlook Today

Here's how	Here's why
1 Display Outlook Today	Click your email account name in the Folder pane.
2 Click as shown	Customize Outlook Today ... **Messages** (On the Outlook Today page.) To open the Customize Outlook Today page in the Outlook window.
3 Check **When starting, go directly to Outlook Today**	(In the Startup section.) To specify that you want Outlook Today to be the startup page.
Under Tasks, select **Today's tasks**	In my task list, show me: ⚬ All tasks ⦿ Today's tasks ☐ Include tasks with no due date To specify that only those tasks you have to perform today should appear in the Tasks list.
From the "Show Outlook Today in this style" list, select **Standard (one column)**	Standard ▼ Standard Standard (two column) Standard (one column) Summer Winter A preview of the selected layout appears under the list.

4 Click **Save Changes**	(This link appears in the upper-right corner of the Customize Outlook Today page.) To save the changes and close the Customize Outlook Today page. Your changes take effect immediately, and the Calendar, Tasks, and Messages headings appear in a single column.
5 Click the **File** tab and choose **Exit**	(Or click the × in the upper-right corner of the Outlook window.) To close Outlook. Next, you'll restart Outlook to verify that the Outlook Today page opens when you start the program.
6 Start Outlook	(Click Start, All Programs, Microsoft Office2013 and choose Outlook 2013.) The Outlook Today page is now the startup page.
7 Click **Customize Outlook Today**	You will restore the default settings for this page.
Uncheck **When starting, go directly to Outlook Today**	
In the Tasks options, select **All tasks**	To display all tasks in the Tasks list.
From the "Show Outlook Today in this style" list, select **Standard**	To use the default three-column style.
Click **Save Changes**	To restore the default settings for this page.

Unit summary: Getting started

Topic A
In this topic, you learned how to **start Outlook 2013**. You also learned about the various **window elements**, including the Quick Access toolbar, the Ribbon, and the Folder pane. You learned how to switch from the Mail view to other views, such as Calendar, Contacts, and Tasks. Next, you learned how to access the default Outlook folders by using the **Folders** Navigation bar menu option. Then you used the **Reading pane** to view message contents.

Topic B
In this topic, you learned that **Outlook Today** is a folder that displays your events, appointments, meetings, and tasks planned for the day. You also learned how to **customize** the Calendar, Tasks, and Messages sections of Outlook Today and change the layout of the Outlook Today page.

Review questions

1 In addition to sending and receiving email messages, what other activities can you do in Outlook?

2 Which of the following is not an Outlook item?

A An email message

B A note

C A contact

D The Ribbon

3 Which pane contains the Navigation bar that enables you to display the Calendar instead of your Inbox?

4 Which default view would you use to access your Contacts folder and a link to connect to a social network?

A Mail

B People

C Tasks

D Contacts

5 What would you use to take a quick look at your Task list from within Mail view, without changing to the Task view?

A Quick glance

B Switch view

C Task peek

D Mail peek

6 Which default folder stores messages that have been identified as spam?

   A Inbox

   B Deleted Items

   C Junk E-mail

   D Drafts

7 True or false? On the Ribbon, the commands available on a tab depend on which view is active.

8 Which pane displays the contents of a mail item?

9 What is Outlook Today?

Independent practice activity

In this activity, you'll customize the Outlook Today page.

1 Customize the Outlook Today page to show the following folders in the Messages section: Deleted Items, Inbox, Junk Email, Outbox, and Sent Items. (*Hint:* In the Outlook Today pane, click Customize Outlook Today.)

2 Customize the Outlook Today page to be displayed in the Summer style.

3 Save the changes you made in Outlook Today.

4 Dock the Calendar Peek to the Outlook Today page.

5 Close Microsoft Office Outlook 2013.

6 Start Microsoft Office Outlook 2013.

7 Restore the default home page for the Outlook Today page.

   To do so, right-click Student##@outlanderspices.com in the Folder pane and choose Data File Properties. Click the Home Page tab, click Restore Defaults, and click OK.

8 Switch to the Folder view and locate your Junk E-mail folder. (*Hint:* Click the Ellipse button from the Navigation bar and select Folders.)

9 Return to the default Mail view.

Unit 2
Email basics

Complete this unit, and you'll know how to:

A Use the Inbox to preview and read messages.

B Create and send messages, and work with automation and formatting features.

C Reply to messages, forward messages, and delete and restore messages.

D Preview, open, read, forward, and save file attachments, and compress images in attachments.

E Customize page setup options for printing, and print messages and attachments.

Topic A: Reading messages

Explanation

You can use Outlook to view, reply to, and forward messages you receive. When you receive an email message, you can save it as a file or forward it to other users. You can also delete email messages and restore deleted messages.

The Inbox

By default, all messages you receive are stored in the Inbox folder. This is one of the most frequently used folders in Outlook. You can read messages stored in the Inbox. You can also create and send messages, and reply to messages. The Message list displays the Folder Contents list. The Reading pane is used to view messages.

The message header

The header of an email message contains *meta-information*, that is, information about the email message. Header details are shown in the Message list as well as in the Reading pane. Header details include:

- **Sender** — Tells you who sent the message.
- **Subject** — Indicates the message's subject, if the sender provided this information. This helps you identify the content of messages.
- **Sending date** — Displays the date and time the message was sent; these are typically close to when you received it.

Messages in the Message list are marked with various icons that help you identify your Inbox contents at a glance. The following table lists these icons and their meanings:

Icon	Description
✉	A message that's been read and replied to
✉	A message that's been read and forwarded
📎	A message with a file attachment
⚑	A flagged message

Additionally, a category indicator icon is shown for each message. By default, messages are uncategorized, so the box-shaped icon is white. You can assign a category, in which case the icon will be blue, red, or one of the other available colors.

Do it!

A-1: Exploring the Inbox

Here's how	Here's why
1 Select **Inbox**	(In the Folder pane.) To view your Outlook Inbox.
Click the **Home** tab	If necessary.
2 Observe the commands on the Home tab	It has mail-specific buttons.
3 Observe the status bar	It shows the total number of messages in the Inbox.
4 Examine the email messages	
	Each message shows the name of the sender (Instructor), the subject of the message, and a preview of the message contents. The Message list also indicates whether you have read the message (black text), the date the message was received, and a flag, if you've flagged the message.
5 Select the message with the subject "Welcome to Outlook 2013"	
6 Observe the Reading pane	The Reading pane shows the content of the message that is selected in the Message list.
Examine the message header	In addition to showing the subject, sender, and date, the Reading pane shows who the message was sent to.

Previewing and reading messages

Explanation
All new messages are delivered to the Inbox. Messages that have not been read appear with blue text for the subject and date. Messages that have been read appear in regular text.

You can read messages in two ways:

- Previewing
- Reading

Previewing messages

By default, you can preview the first line of a message in the Message list. To preview more of a message, you can select it in the Message list to show its contents in the Reading pane.

Reading messages

To read a message, you open it in a new window. To do so, double-click the message in the Message list. Some people prefer to hide the Reading pane and read email messages in a separate window. Doing so provides more screen space for the message, because the Folder pane is not included in the Message window.

As shown in Exhibit 2-1, a Message window contains its own title bar and Ribbon (though not a status bar), as well as sections dedicated to the message header and contents. An additional bar, the People Pane, is present in the Message window, just as it is in the main Outlook window.

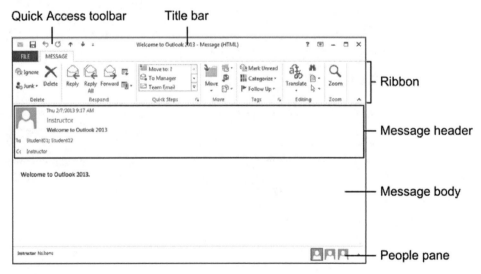

Exhibit 2-1: A received message

Working with the Quick Access toolbar

The Quick Access toolbar contains a selection of commonly used buttons. The default buttons are (from left to right) Save, Undo, Repeat/Redo, Previous item, Next item, and Customize. You can customize the Quick Access toolbar to include buttons for additional commands.

To the left of the Quick Access toolbar is the Control-menu icon. Click it to display the Control menu, which you can use to close the window or otherwise manipulate the window itself.

Closing the message window

To close a message window, you can do any of the following:

- Click the Control-menu icon and choose Close.
- Click the Close button—the "×" in the window's upper-right corner.
- Press Alt+F4.

Do it!

A-2:   Previewing and reading a message

Here's how	Here's why
1 Select a message	(In the Message list.) To preview its contents in the Reading pane.
2 Double-click a message	To open the message in a new window.
3 Examine the Ribbon	
	In addition to the Reply, Reply All, and Forward buttons, the Ribbon contains tools for managing messages and junk email and for tracking and editing messages.
4 Close the message window	Click the Close button.

Topic B: Creating and sending messages

This topic covers the following Microsoft Office Specialist exam objectives for Outlook 2013.

#	Objective
2.1	**Create a Message**
2.1.1	Create messages
2.1.5	Add cc and bcc to messages
2.2	**Format a Message**
2.2.1	Format text

Explanation

Email provides a convenient way to communicate with colleagues and friends. To create a message, click the New Email button on the Home tab. A blank untitled Message window opens, as shown in Exhibit 2-2.

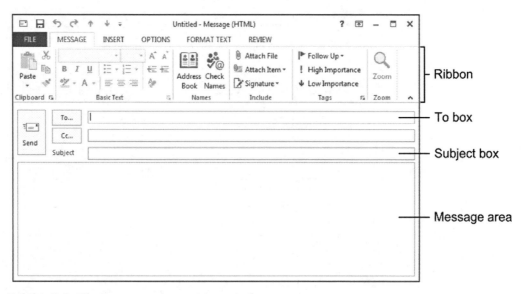

Exhibit 2-2: The message composition window

The following table describes the components of a new Message window.

Component	Used to...
To box	Enter the email addresses of all the people to whom you want to send the message. To send a message to multiple recipients, separate the email addresses with semicolons.
Cc box	Enter the email addresses of all the people to whom you want to send a copy of the message. Officially, cc stands for "carbon copy," a holdover from the days of the typewriter and carbon paper. A more modern interpretation might be "courtesy copy."
Subject box	Type a word or phrase that describes the message.
Message area	Type your message.
Ribbon	Perform various actions, such as sending messages, attaching files, and flagging messages. You can also use buttons here to apply styles, fonts, and other formatting to your message text.

The Bcc box

Recipients can see who a message is sent to by looking at the email header in their Outlook window. This is also true when you include a recipient on the cc line. However, you can send a "blind carbon copy" (bcc) to a recipient. He or she will receive the copy, but none of the other recipients will see his or her name on the To or Cc lines.

By default, a new message window does not include a Bcc box. To add the Bcc box to a message you're composing, click the Options tab on the Ribbon, and in the Show Fields group, click Show Bcc.

Selecting the message format

By default, new messages are composed in HTML format. HTML formatting in a message enables you to apply character and paragraph formats to your message's body text (not to its subject line). You can also compose messages as plain text or Rich Text.

Plain-text messages cannot contain any formatting, such as bold or italics. However, plain-text messages are the smallest in size and most universally supported across various computer platforms and email programs. Rich Text formatting is compatible only with Outlook and Exchange. If you use Rich Text and send a message to someone using an email client other than Outlook, the formatting will be lost.

To change the message format for a single message, create the message and click the Format Text tab. Then click Plain Text or Rich Text in the Format group.

To change the default message format for all messages, click the File tab and then click Options. In the left pane of the Outlook Options dialog box, click Mail. From the "Compose messages in this format" list, select the default format you want to use. Click OK.

Sending messages

You can send your message by clicking the Send button in the email header or by pressing Ctrl+Enter. When you do either, the message is transferred to your Outbox folder. Outlook periodically delivers email and downloads new messages. To force Outlook to send and receive email, click Send/Receive All Folders on the Send/Receive tab.

Whenever you are online and receive a new message, a Desktop Alert appears in the notification area on the Windows taskbar.

Do it!

B-1:   Creating and sending a message

Here's how	Here's why
1 Verify that the Inbox is active	
2 Click **New Email**	To create a message.
3 In the To box, enter **Student##**	In place of ##, enter your partner's number.
4 Press (TAB)	To move the insertion point to the Cc box. You can enter another email address here to send a copy of the message to that person.
5 In the Cc box, enter your instructor's email address	
6 Click the **Options** tab and observe the Show Fields group	You can use these options to insert the Bcc and From boxes.
Click **Bcc** and observe the message	The Bcc box appears under the Cc box.
7 Click the **Bcc** button again	To hide the Bcc box.
8 In the Subject box, enter **Greetings classmate**	
9 In the message area, enter **This is a message from your classmate.**	

10 Click the **Format Text** tab

    Observe the Format group — You can use these options to send the message in HTML, plain text, or Rich Text format. The default is HTML.

11 Be prepared to watch the Outbox folder, which is located in the Folder pane

    Click **Send** — (To the left of the To, Cc, and Subject boxes.) To send the message.

    Observe the Outbox folder — Briefly, a "[1]" should appear after the folder's name. Outlook then transmits your message, removing it from the Outbox.

12 Observe the message from your partner

> ◢ **Today**
>
> **Student02**
> **Greetings classmate**   4:12 PM
> This is a message from your

    It will appear in your Inbox.

    Select the message — To preview it in the Reading pane.

Automation features

Explanation

Microsoft Outlook includes various automation features that help you more easily manage your communications. These include:

- Address lookup and completion
- Word editor integration

Address lookup and completion

When you manually enter names in the To and Cc boxes, Outlook automatically checks your address books for the names. Address books contain the names of people with whom you frequently communicate. If the name you're entering is one you've previously used, Outlook will suggest the matching name or names.

You can either continue typing the name or select it from the shortcut menu. Pressing Tab or Enter will select the first name in the list. You can also press Ctrl+K or click Check Names (on the Ribbon) to look up matching names in your address book, even those names to whom you haven't sent messages recently. Outlook displays the results in a dialog box; double-click a name to enter it in the To or Cc box.

Word editor integration

By default, Outlook uses Microsoft Word components within the message composition window. It's as if the message area box were a mini Word document. This enables you to take advantage of Word's editing features, such as AutoCorrect, AutoComplete, inline spelling and grammar correction, and more. For example, as you type, Outlook (using Word components) automatically checks the spelling of your text. You'll see the same red, wavy underlines beneath misspelled words that you do when typing a report. You can also use Word's AutoComplete features to ease the entry of common items, such as dates.

Do it!

B-2: Working with automation features

Here's how	Here's why
1 Open a new Message window	Click New Email.
2 In the To box, enter **S**	A list appears, showing the names, starting with S, to whom you have recently sent email.
Press (TAB)	Outlook automatically completes the name based on the email address that you used earlier. Notice that Student## is entered in the box automatically.
In the Subject box, enter **Testing Outlook automation**	
3 Press (TAB)	To move the insertion point into the message area.

4 Type **today**

   Press (SPACEBAR)   Notice that the "today" you typed is converted
                                            to "Today" because of Word's AutoCorrect
                                            feature.

5 Type **is** and press (SPACEBAR)

   Type the first four letters of
   today's weekday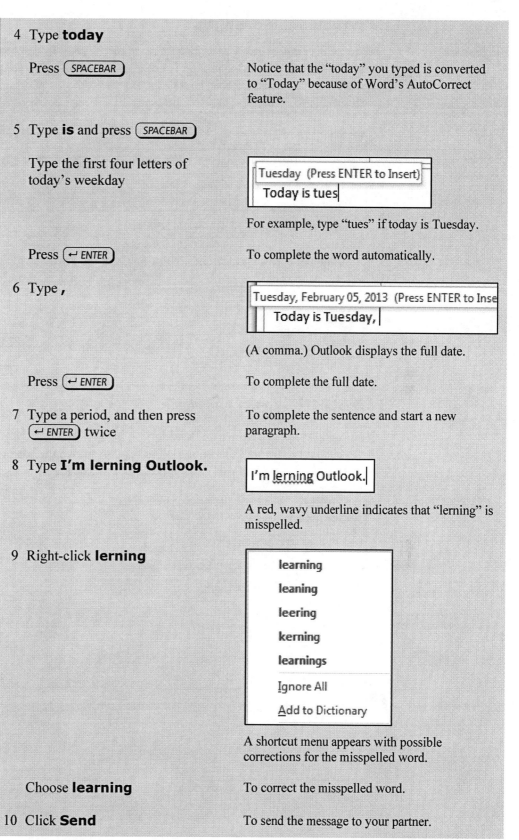

                                            Tuesday (Press ENTER to Insert)
                                            Today is tues

                                            For example, type "tues" if today is Tuesday.

   Press (↵ ENTER)   To complete the word automatically.

6 Type **,**

                                            Tuesday, February 05, 2013 (Press ENTER to Inse
                                            Today is Tuesday,

                                            (A comma.) Outlook displays the full date.

   Press (↵ ENTER)   To complete the full date.

7 Type a period, and then press   To complete the sentence and start a new
   (↵ ENTER) twice   paragraph.

8 Type **I'm lerning Outlook.**

                                            I'm lerning Outlook.

                                            A red, wavy underline indicates that "lerning" is
                                            misspelled.

9 Right-click **lerning**

                                            learning

                                            leaning

                                            leering

                                            kerning

                                            learnings

                                            Ignore All

                                            Add to Dictionary

                                            A shortcut menu appears with possible
                                            corrections for the misspelled word.

   Choose **learning**   To correct the misspelled word.

10 Click **Send**   To send the message to your partner.

Formatting messages

Explanation   When you create or reply to a message, you might want to emphasize some important text. You can do this by changing its color, size, or font or by applying underlining or italics. You can use the Basic Text group on the Ribbon's Message tab, shown in Exhibit 2-3, to format the text in a message.

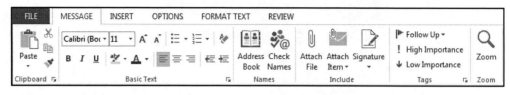

Exhibit 2-3: The Message tab on the Ribbon in a new Message window

For additional styles and formatting options, use the Format Text tab, shown in Exhibit 2-4.

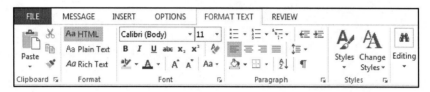

Exhibit 2-4: The Format Text tab

You can also use the Mini toolbar to format the text in a message. When you select the text you want to format, the Mini toolbar appears above the selected text, as shown in Exhibit 2-5. If you point away from the selected text, the Mini toolbar will disappear.

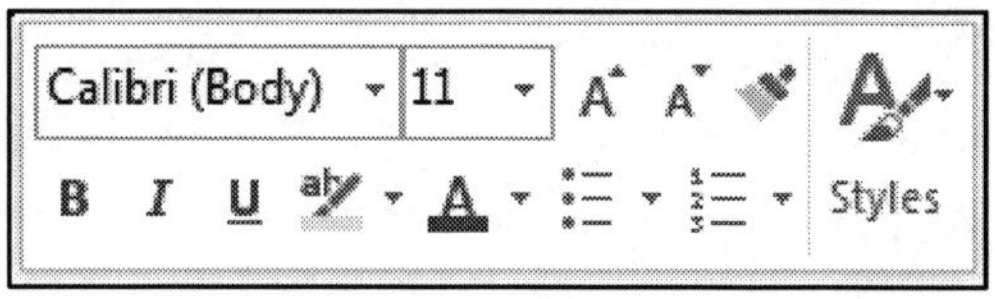

Exhibit 2-5: The Mini toolbar

Do it!

B-3: Formatting a message

Here's how	Here's why
1 Open a new Message window	Click New Email.
2 In the To box, enter the name of your partner	To address the message to your partner.
In the Subject box, enter **Venue for the class**	
Press (TAB)	To move the insertion point into the message area.
In the message area, type as shown (including the misspelling)	The venu for today's class is: Outlander Spices, 1170 Blackhorse Ave, Texas
3 Select the first line of text, as shown	The venu for today's class is: You'll format this text.
4 From the Font Size list, select **12**	The list is in the Basic Text group on the Message tab.
From the Font list, select **Arial Black**	
Deselect the text	(Click anywhere in the message area.) The font and size of the message text have changed.
5 Select **Outlander Spices** and click [B]	(The Bold button is on the Ribbon.) To make the selected text bold.
Deselect the text, and click at the end of the text	To see the changes and place the insertion point at the end of the text.
6 Press (↵ ENTER)	
Type **Time:** and press (SPACEBAR)	
Type **10:30 AM tomorrow**	To specify the time of the class.
7 Double-click **tomorrow** but don't move the mouse pointer afterward	The Mini toolbar appears as a semi-transparent pop-up.
Point to the Mini toolbar	It changes from semi-transparent to fully visible.
From the Font Size list, select **14**	On the Mini toolbar.
8 Deselect the text	If necessary.

Checking spelling and grammar in messages

Explanation

By default, Microsoft Word checks spelling and grammar automatically as you type. If you misspell a word, a wavy red line appears under the word. If Word finds a grammatical problem, a wavy green line appears under the word or words. If you mistype a word and the result is not a misspelling (for example, "form" instead of "from"), the spelling checker will not flag the word.

You can postpone proofing your message until after you finish writing it. To start checking the spelling, click the Review tab and then click Spelling & Grammar in the Proofing group, or press F7. The same Spelling and Grammar dialog box you would see in Word is opened, as shown in Exhibit 2-6. (The language your system is configured to use will be displayed after the dialog box's name. In the exhibit, U.S. English is the default language.)

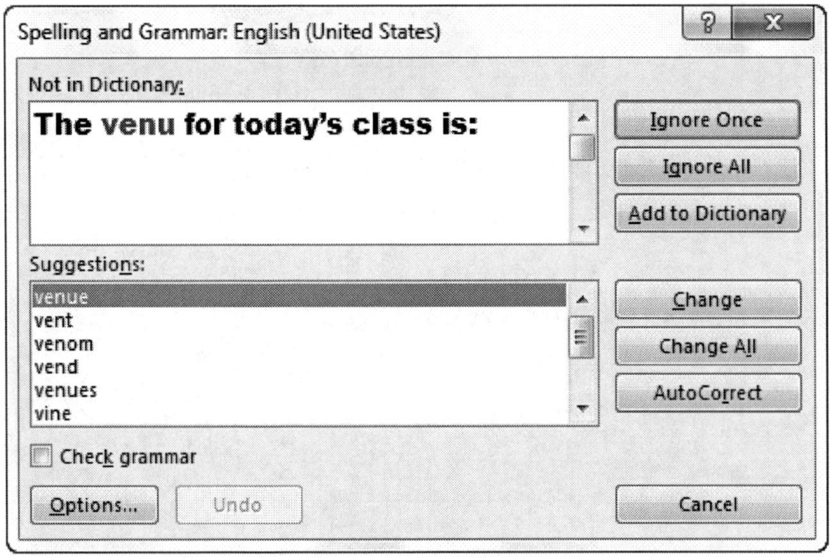

Exhibit 2-6: The Spelling and Grammar dialog box

The misspelled word is shown in the Not in Dictionary box, and suggestions are shown in the Suggestions list. Select the appropriately spelled word and click Change to change a single occurrence of the misspelled word, or click Change All to change all occurrences of that word. You can also click Ignore Once to ignore one instance or click Ignore All to ignore all instances of a specific word.

Do it!

B-4: Checking a message's spelling

Here's how	Here's why
1 Click the **Review** tab	
2 Click the indicated button	ABC ✓ Spelling & Grammar
	To open the Spelling and Grammar dialog box. This dialog box opens only when there is an incorrect word in the message.
3 Observe the Spelling and Grammar dialog box	It displays the incorrect word ("venu") in red and prompts you to correct it by selecting a word from the Suggestions list.
From the Suggestions list, select **venue**	(If necessary.) This is the correct spelling.
4 Click **Change**	A message box appears, informing you that the spelling and grammar check is complete.
Click **OK**	To close the message box. Notice that "Venu" has changed to "Venue."
5 Send the message	
6 Check for new messages	If necessary, click Send/Receive.
7 Select the message with the subject **Venue for the class**	(Click the message in the Inbox.) The contents of the message appear in the Reading pane. The message includes the formatting your partner applied.

Paste options

Explanation   The various applications in Office 2013 provide you with a number of ways to paste content into a document, and Outlook 2013 is no exception. When you click the Paste button's arrow, you're presented with a Paste Options menu, as shown in Exhibit 2-7. The paste options will vary, depending on what text you've cut or copied to the Clipboard. When you point to each option, you'll see an example of what its result will look like in the message body.

Exhibit 2-7: Paste options

The typical paste options are described in the following table.

Option	Name and description
	Use Destination Theme — Uses the theme, including fonts, defined for your e-mail messages. This option will format the pasted content so it looks like the current message text.
	Keep Source Formatting — Keeps the formatting used in the document from which you copied the content. When you choose this option, the content will look like it did in the original document or Web page.
	Merge Formatting — Outlook will incorporate both the source and the message format.
	Keep Text Only — Only the text will be pasted; the text will not be formatted.
Paste Special...	Paste Special — Opens the Paste Special dialog box, shown in Exhibit 2-8. You can use this dialog box to paste text as any of the following: • A Microsoft Office object, whose content you can edit by using the original Office application, such as Word or Excel • Formatted text (RTF) • Plain text only • HTML • Unformatted Unicode Text, which is a text-only format You can also paste the item as a link to the original document, using any of the formats described above. A link between the source and the message content will allow you to update the message content if any changes are made in the same content in the source (for example, text in a Word document or numbers in an Excel spreadsheet are changed).

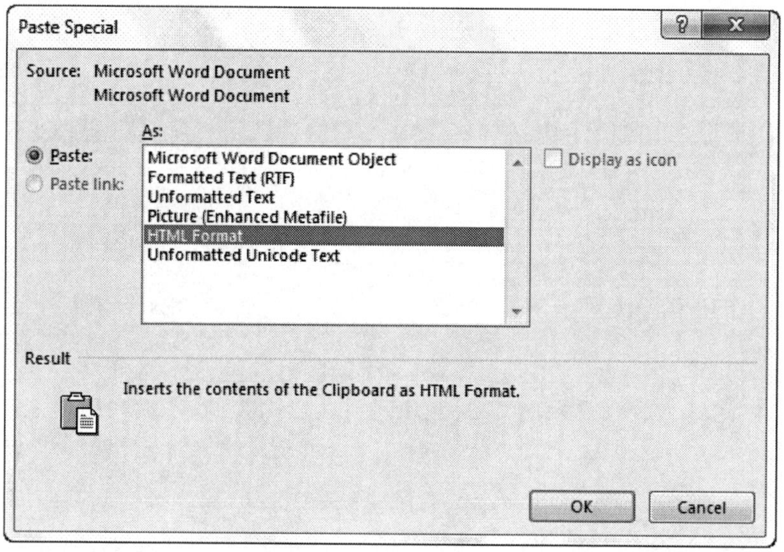

Exhibit 2-8: Paste Special options

Do it!

B-5:   Pasting content from an Office document

The files for this activity are in Student Data folder **Unit 2\Topic B**.

Here's how	Here's why
1 Create a message and address it to your partner	
Type the subject **Sales for Last Two Quarters**	
2 In the message area, type **Here's a quick summary.**	
Press (↵ ENTER) twice	To create line breaks.
3 From Windows Explorer, open Analysis	To open the source document in Word.
Select **Sales Analysis...** and the table beneath it	
Click 🖹	(The Copy button.) To copy the text.
Close Word	
4 Switch to Outlook	If necessary. If you're asked to keep the last item you copied, click Yes.
Click the Paste button's arrow	To display the paste options.

5	Point to	(Use Destination Theme.) To see what the text would look like using the current theme in Outlook.
6	Point to	(Keep Source Formatting.) To see the text using the formatting from the Word document.
7	Point to	(Merge Formatting.) To see the text with both Outlook and Word formatting merged.
8	Point to	(Keep Text Only.) To show the text only, without any formatting. The table is broken.
9	Choose **Paste Special...**	To open the Paste Special dialog box. You can paste the text or a link to the source text in the Word document.
	Select **Microsoft Word Document Object** and click **OK**	
10	Double-click the table in the Outlook message body	To open the text for editing in Word. The Paste Special option you chose allows you to open the text in the original application if you want to change it before you send the message.
11	Close Word and send the message	
	Click Send Anyway	(If necessary.) To close the Attachment Reminder dialog box.
	Close Windows Explorer	If necessary.

Topic C: Working with messages

This topic covers the following Microsoft Office Specialist exam objectives for Outlook 2013.

#	Objective
1.1	**Customize Outlook Settings**
1.1.1	Include original messages with all reply messages
2.1	**Create a Message**
2.1.2	Forward messages
2.1.3	Delete messages
2.1.7	Reply to all
2.1.8	Reply to sender only
2.2	**Format a Message**
2.2.2	Insert hyperlinks

Explanation

Outlook provides a variety of tools for managing your email messages. Using Outlook, you can:

- Reply to messages
- Forward messages
- Delete and restore email messages

Replying to messages

When you open a received message, Outlook provides two reply buttons in the Respond group on the Ribbon:

- **Reply** — Creates a return message addressed only to the sender.
- **Reply All** — Creates a return message addressed to the sender and everyone who received a carbon copy of the original message.

Reply messages, by default, contain the original message text. This is useful when you need to refer to the original message. Also, when you type any text in the reply Message window, the text appears in blue so you can distinguish between your reply and the original message text.

Email etiquette suggests that you should trim the original message text to just the pertinent portions. Many people consider it rude to include screen after screen of prior text in a reply.

To send a reply:

1 Preview or open the message to which you want to reply.
2 Click Reply. This opens the reply in the Reading pane, with the name of the original sender in the To box. The reply message uses the subject of the original message with "RE:" added as a prefix.
3 Type your reply in the message area.
4 Click Send.

Do it!

C-1: Replying to a message

Here's how	Here's why
1 Select the message with the subject **Greetings classmate**	(Click the message in your Inbox.) You'll reply to this message.
2 Click **Reply**	To show the reply Message in the Reading pane and compose a reply.
Observe the reply in the Reading pane	

	To...	student01@outlanderspices.com
	Cc...	
Send	Subject	RE: Greetings classmate

	The To box contains the name of the message sender. The Subject box displays the same subject, but with RE: added as a prefix.
3 Verify that the insertion point is in the first line of the message area	You'll type your reply here.
4 Type **Thank you**	
Press (↵ ENTER)	The message text is blue.
5 Move to the next line	Press Enter.
Type your name	
6 Send the message	Click Send. The Reading pane returns to the message view.
7 Click as shown	

> Student02
> Greetings classmate   4:12 PM
> This is a message from your

8 Observe the message in the Reading pane	

> Greetings classmate
> To Student01
> Cc Instructor
> ❶ You replied to this message on 2/9/2013 3:06 PM.

The message indicates the action taken on the message, along with the date and time. In this case, the action was replying to a message.

9 Observe the Message list	
	The original message now has an icon showing that you have replied to the message.
10 In the Folder pane, click **Sent Items**	To open the Sent Items folder. The reply you sent appears here. Any message you send will be stored in this folder.
11 Select your Inbox	Next, you'll use the Reply All option.
12 Select the message with the subject **Greetings classmate**	You'll send a reply to the sender and to anyone who received a Cc.
13 Click **Reply All**	To open a reply Message in the Reading pane.
14 Observe the Reply message	The To box contains the name of the sender of the message, and the Cc box contains the name of the person who received a copy of the original message. (In this case, Instructor should be listed on the Cc line.)
15 Type **Hello!**	In the message area.
16 Click **Send**	To send the reply to the sender and to the person who was copied on the original message.

Forwarding messages

Explanation

When you receive a message that other people need to know about, you can forward it to them. To forward a message:

1 Open or select the message.

2 Click Forward.

3 Enter the recipient's name in the To box.

4 Click Send.

By default, when you forward a message, you're really creating a new message. And in that new message, the entire original message is included in the body text, with the insertion point at the top of the new message, above the original message text. You can change this default behavior by using the Outlook Options dialog box.

To open the dialog box, click the File tab and then click Options. In the left pane, click Mail to display the mail properties that you can configure. Scroll to find the "Replies and forwards" section, shown in Exhibit 2-9. Using these settings, you can configure the following forwarding options:

- Open the message in a new window after you click Forward.

- Close the original message window after you click Forward. This can help you clean up the desktop by closing an unnecessary window.

- Insert your name before your comments if you make any comments inside the original message text.

- Configure the appearance of the original message text in the body of your forwarded message.

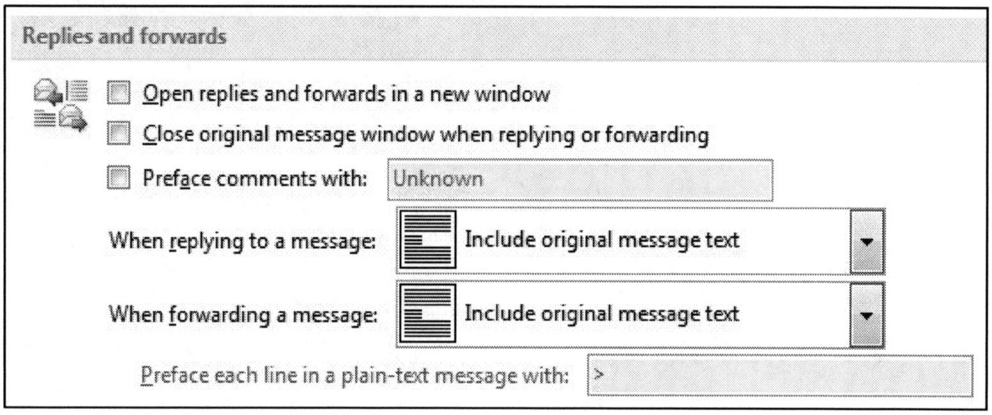

Exhibit 2-9: Forwarding options

Do it!

C-2:   Forwarding a message

Here's how	Here's why
1 Click the **File** tab and then click **Options**	To open the Outlook Options dialog box.
2 In the left pane, click **Mail**	
Scroll to the "Replies and forwards" section	
3 Observe the settings	You can configure Outlook to open the message in a new window when you click Forward, close the original message window when you click Forward, preface your inline comments with your user name, and configure how original message text appears in your forwarded message.
Click **Cancel**	
4 Select the message with the subject **Venue for the class**	In the Inbox Message list.
5 Click ![Forward]	The message opens in the Reading pane. The subject of the message is the original subject, with the prefix FW: added.
6 In the To box, enter **Student*XX***	(Where *XX* is the number of a classmate other than your partner.) To forward the message to the specified user.
7 In the message area, type **I thought you might find this useful.**	Notice that the text you type appears in blue.
8 Send the message	
9 Open the Sent Items folder	(Click Sent Items in the Folder pane.) The message you forwarded appears in the Sent Items Message list.

Hyperlinks

Explanation

Sharing favorite or useful Web sites is a common use of email. You might send friends links to sites you think are funny or informative, or send colleagues links to sites providing valuable information for projects or day-to-day operations. Sharing a hyperlink is as easy as performing a copy and paste.

First, in your Web browser, select the text in the Address bar. Either press Ctrl+C, or right-click the selected text and choose Copy. Then, in Outlook, create a message and address it to your intended recipients. When you get to the body of the message, click the Paste button's arrow and choose the Keep Text Only option.

You can also insert a hyperlink from within Outlook by using the Insert Hyperlink dialog box, shown in Exhibit 2-10. This dialog box offers several options not available when you just copy and paste a hyperlink.

- You can label the hyperlink with a title and create a custom ScreenTip for it.
- You can create a link to a file, a Web page, a location within a file or Web page, or an email address.

To open the Insert Hyperlink dialog box, click the Insert tab and then click Hyperlink in the Links group. Or you can right-click a blank area of a message and choose Hyperlink.

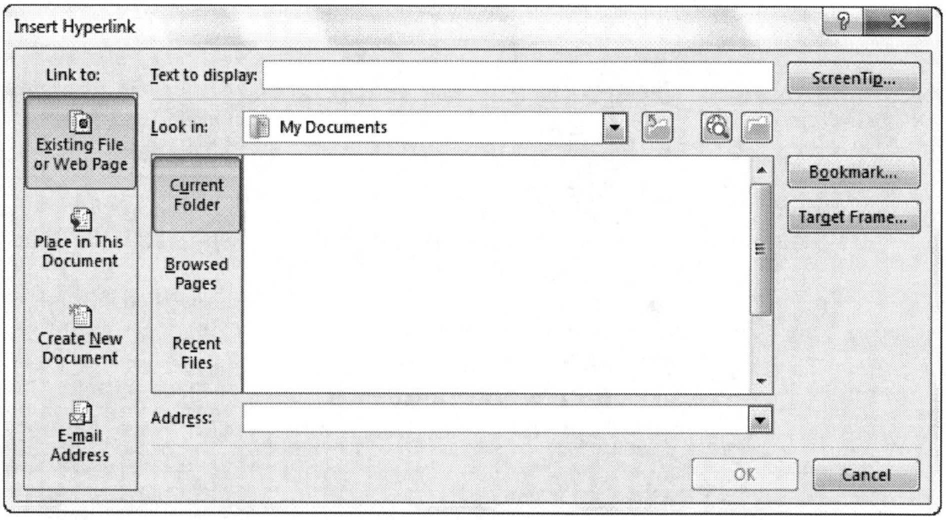

Exhibit 2-10: Inserting a hyperlink

Do it!

C-3: Inserting a hyperlink

Here's how	Here's why
1 Open Internet Explorer and navigate to **www.microsoft.com\outlook**	
	To visit a Web page that you'll link to in an email message.
If prompted to set up Internet Explorer, close the dialog box	

2 Click in the Address bar

`http://office.microsoft.com/en-us/outlook`

To select the text. You'll see the address changed to the correct address for Microsoft's Outlook home page.

Right-click the selected text and choose **Copy**

3 In Outlook, click **New Email**

On the Home tab.

In the To box, enter your partner's email address

In the Subject box, type **Interesting Outlook information**

4 Right-click in the message body, and under Paste Options, click **Keep Text Only**

To paste the hyperlink into the new message.

5 Press (⏎ ENTER) twice

To create two blank lines.

6 Click the **Insert** tab, and in the Links group, click ⊕ Hyperlink

To open the Insert Hyperlink dialog box.

7 Observe the dialog box

In the Link to list, you can select what you want to link to, including a file or Web page, a place in a document you're working on, a new document, or an email address. You can use the "Text to display" box to label the hyperlink, and use the ScreenTip button to create a ScreenTip.

8 In the Link to list, verify that **Existing File or Web Page** is selected

In the details pane, click **Browsed Pages**

Select the **Email and Calendar Software | Microsoft Outlook – Office.com** link

The "Text to display" box contains the page's title. The Address box contains the Web address of the page you visited earlier in this task.

9 Click **OK**

To close the Insert Hyperlink dialog box.

Observe the link

It has the title you saw in the "Text to display" box. If you compare it to the link you copied into the message, you can see that it looks a little more professional than a plain Web address.

10 Click **Send**

To send the message to your partner.

Deleting and restoring messages

Explanation

You can delete messages that you don't need any longer. To delete a message, you select it and then either click the Delete button (on the Home tab) or press the Delete key.

Deleted messages are not immediately removed. Instead, they are moved to the Deleted Items folder. This means you can recover accidentally deleted items by moving them out of the Deleted Items folder into another folder. You can also select a message, click the Home tab, click Move (in the Move group), and choose Other Folder. In the Move Items dialog box, select the folder you want to move the message to and click OK.

To permanently delete an item, you must empty the Deleted Items folder. To do so, select that folder, click the Folder tab, and click Empty Folder. You can also right-click the Deleted Items folder and choose Empty Folder.

If you're using a Microsoft Exchange Server account, messages might still be recoverable even after you empty the Deleted Items folder. Click the Folder tab and then click Recover Deleted Items. Select the messages you want to recover, and click the Recover Selected Items button. The messages will appear in the Deleted Items folder. The Exchange administrator controls how long deleted messages will be recoverable.

Do it!

C-4: Deleting and restoring a message

Here's how	Here's why
1 Open the Inbox folder	Click Inbox in the Folder pane.
2 Select the message with the subject **Your second message**	You'll delete this message.
3 Click Delete	(On the Home tab.) To delete the message. It is removed from the Message list.
4 Select the Instructor's message with the subject **Welcome to Outlook 2013**	
Press (DELETE)	To delete the message.
5 Open the Deleted Items folder	(Click Deleted Items in the Folder pane.) The deleted messages appear in this folder, which stores all of the deleted messages.
6 Drag the **Welcome to Outlook 2013** message to the Inbox folder in the Folder pane	To restore the deleted message.
Select the **Inbox** folder	The message has been restored to your Inbox.

7 Select the **Deleted Items**
   folder

   Right-click the **Deleted Items**
   text

   Select **Empty Folder**   To remove the message from the Deleted Items
                                              folder. A message box prompts you to confirm
                                              the deletion.

   Click **Yes**   The folder is emptied.

8 Click **Recover Deleted Items**   On the Folder tab.

   Select the message with the subject
   Your second message

   Click [icon]   After a moment or two, the message appears in
                                             the Deleted Items folder again.

9 Click the **File** tab and then click   To open the Outlook Options dialog box. You'll
   Options   configure Outlook to automatically delete items
                                             from your Deleted Items folder when you close
                                             Outlook.

   Click **Advanced**

   In the "Outlook start and exit"
   section, check **Empty Deleted
   Items folders when exiting
   Outlook**

   Click **OK**   To close the Outlook Options dialog box.

10 Select the **Inbox** folder

Topic D: Handling attachments

This topic covers the following Microsoft Office Specialist exam objectives for Outlook 2013.

#	Objective
1.3	**Print and Save Information in Outlook**
1.3.3	Save message attachments
1.3.4	Preview attachments
2.1	**Create a Message**
2.1.4	Adding/removing message attachments
2.2	**Format a Message**
2.2.4	Insert images

Explanation

In addition to sending a standard email message, you can add an attachment to the message. When you receive an email message that includes an attachment, you can preview or save the attachment. You can also forward the attachment to others.

Attach a file to a new message

You can attach any type of file to an email message in order to send the file to the recipient. For example, you can send Word, graphics, sound, and movie files as attachments. You can attach a single file or multiple files to a message. The Attached box displays the name and size of each attachment.

To attach a file:

1   Create a message.
2   Click the Attach File button in the Include group on the Ribbon.
3   Select the file you want to insert, and click Insert. The Attached box, listing the attached file, appears under the Subject box.

By default, Outlook blocks potentially unsafe attachments, such as EXE and VBS files, which can contain viruses. If you attach a file with an extension that might be blocked by Outlook, you will be asked whether you want to send a potentially unsafe attachment. If you send the attachment anyway, it might be blocked by the recipient's Outlook program or antivirus software.

Forward a message that contains an attachment

You can forward a message that contains an attachment by opening the message and clicking Forward. By default, the file is attached to the message. Type your note, address the message, and click Send.

You can also forward a message and add an attachment. To do so:

1   Open the message you want to forward.
2   Click the Forward button in the Respond group on the Ribbon.
3   Click the Attach File button in the Include group on the Ribbon.
4   Select the file you want to insert, and click Insert. The Attached box, listing the attached file, appears under the Subject box.

Do it!   ## D-1:   Sending and forwarding attachments

The files for this activity are in Student Data folder **Unit 2\Topic D**.

Here's how	Here's why
1 Click the **Home** tab	
2 Click **New Email**	
Address the message to your partner	In the To box, type your partner's email address.
Enter the subject as **Sales Report**	
3 In the message area, type **I am sending the West Coast sales report.**	
4 Click [Attach File icon]	(In the Include group on the Ribbon.) To open the Insert File dialog box.
5 Navigate to the current topic folder	Student Data folder Unit 2\Topic D.
Select **Analysis**	(If necessary.) Analysis is a Word document that contains a table and a graph showing the growth of sales.
Click **Insert**	

Send

To... Student02@outlanderspices.com

Cc...

Subject Sales Report

Attached Analysis.docx (16 KB)

I am sending the West Coast sales report.

	To attach the file. The Attached box appears under the Subject box and displays the name and size of the attachment.
6 Send the message	After a moment, your partner's message will appear in your Inbox. If it doesn't, click Send/Receive on the Send/Receive tab.

7 Observe the new message in your Inbox	**Student02** 📎 **Sales Report** 8:36 PM I am sending the West Coast sales
	The attachment icon (a paperclip) appears to the right of the sender name in the header information.
8 Select the message from your partner	
9 Click **Forward**	The attachment appears in the Attached field.
10 Click ✖	To close the message without sending it.

Resizing images and image attachments

If you are using HTML or the Rich Text format for your messages, you can insert images into the message body or as attachments. If you insert or attach large pictures or several pictures, you might want to resize them to make the message smaller.

Inserting vs. attaching

When you insert an image, it appears within the text of your message, much like a picture you insert in a Word memo appears within the document. An attached image is treated just like an attached document: it is listed in the Attached box when you send the message, and it is not displayed inline.

Resizing image attachments

You can use an image editing program to resize an image before attaching it to your email message. However, Outlook can handle the task for you automatically.

After attaching the image, click the File tab. If necessary, click Info. Then select "Resize large images when I send this message." Outlook will automatically resize the image to a maximum of 1024 × 768 pixels.

Compressing inserted images

After you insert pictures into a message, select an image to display the Picture Tools | Format tab. (This is one of Outlook's *contextual tabs*—tabs that appear only in certain circumstances.) Click the Compress Pictures button, select a compression option, and click OK.

Do it!

D-2: Inserting, attaching, and compressing images

The files for this activity are in Student Data folder **Unit 2\Topic D**.

Here's how	Here's why
1 Create a message	
2 In the To box, enter the name of your partner	
3 In the Subject box, enter **Spice Picture 1**	
In the message area, type **Here's the first spice arrangement picture for the newsletter.**	
4 Click **Attach File**	The Attach File button is in the Include group on the Ribbon.
5 Navigate to the current topic folder	
Point to Spicearrangement1	The image is an approximately 1.3 MB TIF file.
Select **Spicearrangement1**	
Click **Insert**	
6 In the Message window, click the **File** tab	The Info command will be selected by default.
Select **Resize large images when I send this message**	

Image Attachments

Some recipients may not receive this message because of image attachments. Resizing large images may help the message get delivered. Resized images will be a maximum of 1024x768 pixels.

◉ Resize large images when I send this message.
○ Do not resize images.

Click the left-pointing arrow	(In the upper-left corner.) To return to the message window.
7 Click **Send**	The image is resized automatically and the message is delivered.
8 Create a message addressed to your partner	
9 In the Subject box, enter **Spice Picture 2**	

10 In the message area, type **Here's the second arrangement picture.**

    Press (⏎ ENTER)

11 Click the **Insert** tab

    Click **Pictures**

    Navigate to the current topic folder

    Select **Spicearrangement2.tif**   The size of the file is approximately 1.3 MB.

    Click **Insert**   To insert the picture in the body of the message. The Picture Tools | Format tab appears.

12 Click 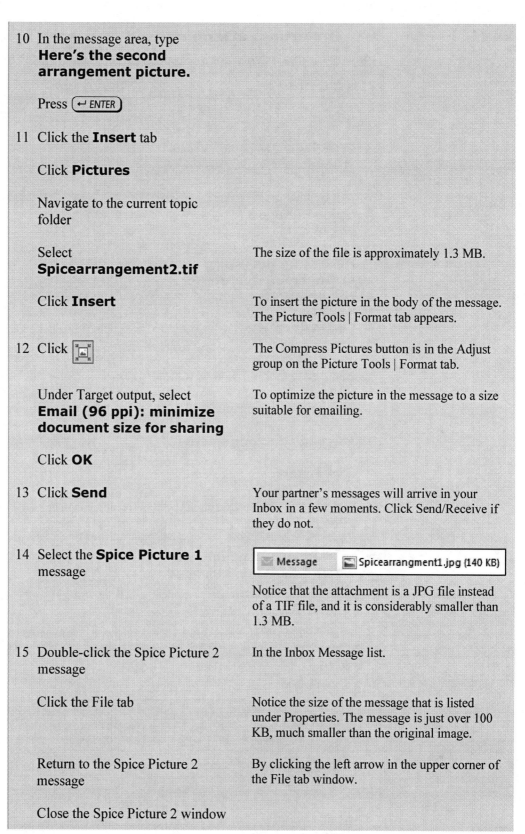   The Compress Pictures button is in the Adjust group on the Picture Tools | Format tab.

    Under Target output, select **Email (96 ppi): minimize document size for sharing**   To optimize the picture in the message to a size suitable for emailing.

    Click **OK**

13 Click **Send**   Your partner's messages will arrive in your Inbox in a few moments. Click Send/Receive if they do not.

14 Select the **Spice Picture 1** message

Message	Spicearrangment1.jpg (140 KB)

    Notice that the attachment is a JPG file instead of a TIF file, and it is considerably smaller than 1.3 MB.

15 Double-click the Spice Picture 2 message   In the Inbox Message list.

    Click the File tab   Notice the size of the message that is listed under Properties. The message is just over 100 KB, much smaller than the original image.

    Return to the Spice Picture 2 message   By clicking the left arrow in the upper corner of the File tab window.

    Close the Spice Picture 2 window

Previewing and saving attachments

Explanation

When you receive a message containing a file attachment, the message will have a paperclip icon in the Message list. The icon appears to the left of the sender's name (as part of the header information). You can view the name and size of the attachment, as shown in Exhibit 2-11, in the header of the Reading pane or in the opened message.

Exhibit 2-11: An attachment

Previewing or opening an attachment

When a message contains an attachment, you can click the attachment's name to preview the file in the Reading pane or message window. You can open the attachment in its associated program by double-clicking the attachment's name. For example, double-clicking a Word document opens Microsoft Word.

Saving an attachment

You can save all attachments or a single attachment to an email message. There are several ways to save an attachment:

- Use the Save As button on the Attachments tab.
- Right-click the attachment and choose Save As.
- Double-click the attachment, and once the attachment is opened in its associated program, save it from within that program.

Do it!

D-3: Previewing and saving an attachment

Here's how	Here's why
1 Select the **Sales Report** message from your partner	To display the message contents in the Reading pane.
2 In the Reading pane, observe the attachment area	✉ Message 📄 Analysis.docx (16 KB) It displays Message text and the name and size of the attachment.
3 In the Reading pane, click the attachment's file name	You'll see the message "Starting Microsoft Word Previewer" in the Reading pane. After a moment, the attachment is displayed inline.
In the Message list, click the message	To display the message again without previewing the attachment.
4 Double-click the attachment's file name	To open the attachment in Microsoft Word. The Opening Mail Attachment dialog box might appear.
5 Close Microsoft Word	To return to Outlook.
6 In the Reading pane, select the attachment	
7 On the Attachments tab, in the Actions group, click **Save As**	
8 Navigate to the current topic folder	Student Data folder Unit 2\Topic D.
Edit the File name box to read **My sales**	To save the attachment with a different name.
Click **Save**	To save the attachment and close the Save As dialog box.
9 Select the **Spice Picture 2** message	(In the Message list.) The image that your partner inserted into that message is immediately visible. It's not an attachment.
10 Right-click the picture	The shortcut menu includes the Save As Picture command. You could click it to save this picture, just like you saved the attachment.
Press (ESC)	To close the shortcut menu.

Topic E: Printing messages and attachments

This topic covers the following Microsoft Office Specialist exam objectives for Outlook 2013.

#	Objective
1.3	**Print and Save Information in Outlook**
1.3.1	Print messages

Explanation

As with other Office documents, you can print Outlook messages. You can also control page settings such as margins, headers and footers, and orientation.

By using the options on the Print page, shown in Exhibit 2-12, you can specify which printer to use. You can also specify the style, the number of copies, and other settings for printouts. Click the File tab and choose Print to display these options.

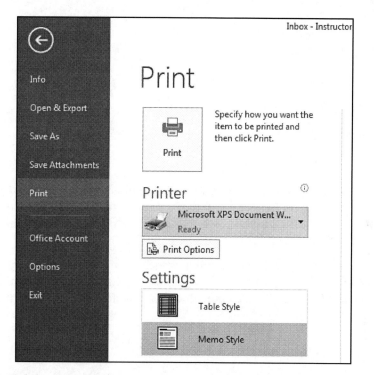

Exhibit 2-12: The Print page

The Print page displays a preview of the way your message will look when printed. From this page, you can specify which printer to print to. Use the Table Style option to print a list of messages in your Inbox (or currently selected folder). Use the Memo Style option to print the open or previewed email message. Click the large Print button at the top of the page to actually print.

To customize the way messages print, you can change the page setup. The Page Setup: Memo Style dialog box is shown in Exhibit 2-13. You can use the Format, Paper, and Header/Footer tabs to specify the fonts, paper source, margins, orientation, and header and footer for the printed message. A header will appear at the top of the page, and the footer will appear at the bottom of the page. A page layout preview appears on the Format tab.

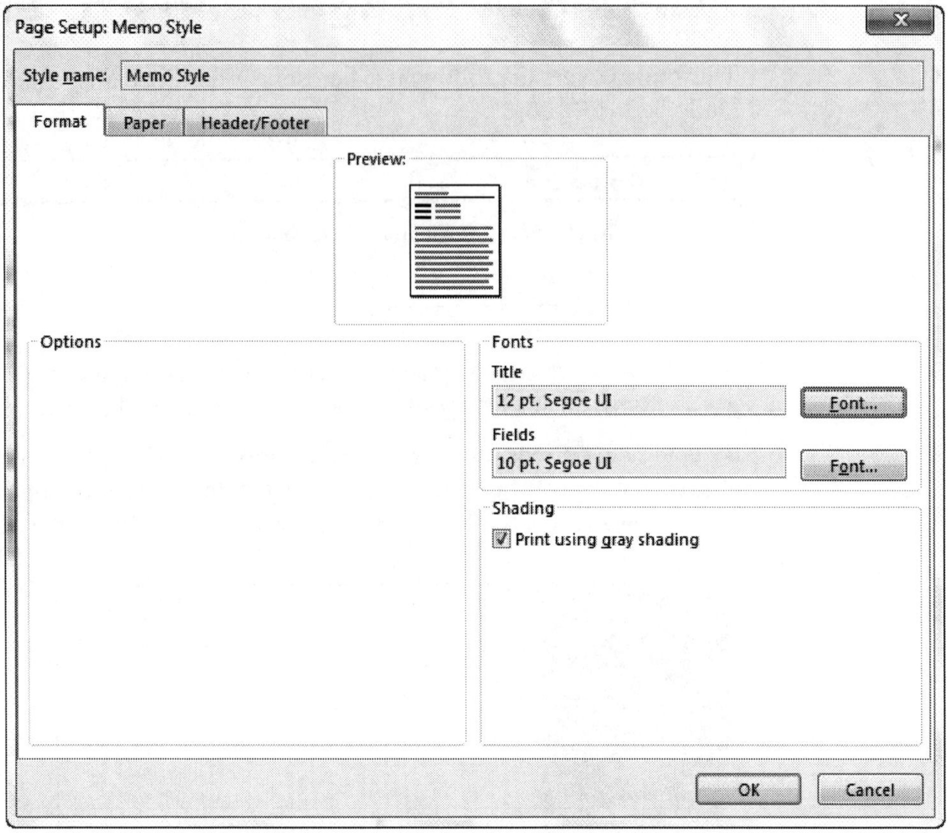

Exhibit 2-13: The Page Setup dialog box

To print a message, you can right-click it in the Inbox and choose Quick Print. The message will print to your default printer, and you won't be able to change any print settings. To print multiple messages, select each message you want to print; then click the File tab and click Print.

To print an attachment, you can double-click it to open it and then print it from within the application. Or you can right-click the attachment in an open message and choose Quick Print to print the attachment without changing any print settings.

Do it!   **E-1:   Printing messages and attachments**

Here's how	Here's why
1 Click **Inbox**	If necessary, to select your Inbox.
Select any message	In your Inbox.
2 Click the **File** tab and then click **Print**	To display the Print page. A large preview of your printout is shown on the right. In the middle are options for selecting the printer and the output style.
3 Click **Table Style**	The preview changes to show that a list of the messages in your Inbox will be printed instead of a single message.
4 Click **Print Options**	To open the Print dialog box. You can use controls in this dialog box to specify which printer to print to, how many copies to print, the range of pages to print, and so forth.
5 Select **Memo Style**	
Click **Page Setup**	To open the Page Setup dialog box.
6 Click the **Paper** tab	Use this tab to specify settings related to paper size and orientation.
7 Click **OK**	
8 Click **Print**	To print the message.
9 Return to the Inbox	
Select two messages	Use Ctrl+click to select them.
10 Click the **File** tab and click **Print**	
11 Preview the messages in the preview pane	
Click **Print**	To print both messages.
12 Open a message with an attachment	
Right-click the attachment and choose **Quick Print**	To print the attachment.

Unit summary: Email basics

Topic A   In this topic, you learned how to work with email messages. You **previewed** a message in the Reading pane and **opened** a message in its own window.

Topic B   In this topic, you **created** and **sent** a message. You used automation features such as AutoComplete and Check Names. In addition, you used the Ribbon and the Mini toolbar to format message text. You also learned how to check the **spelling** and **grammar** in a message.

Topic C   In this topic, you replied to and forwarded messages. You learned that when replying to a message, you can **reply** to the sender alone or **reply to all** people who received the original message. You also learned how to **delete** messages and **restore** deleted messages from the Deleted Items folder.

Topic D   In this topic, you **attached** a file to a message, and you previewed and saved an attachment. Next, you inserted and attached **images** to messages and compressed those images. Then, you previewed, opened, and saved an attachment.

Topic E   In this topic, you learned how to customize the **page setup** when printing messages. You also learned how to **print** a message and an attachment.

Review questions

1 When you are looking at the Message list, what indicates that you've replied to a particular message?

2 When should you use the To line versus the Cc line while addressing an email message?

3 Which feature automatically checks the address book for the message recipient's name?

   A AutoCorrect   C Name-checking

   B AutoComplete   D Spell-checking

4 Which feature automatically enters the recipient's name based on email addresses you've used earlier?

   A AutoCorrect   C Name-checking

   B AutoComplete   D SmartTags

5 What is the difference between using the Reply button and the Reply All button?

6 What is the procedure to attach a file to an email message?

7 In what way does a message's subject change when you forward the message?

8 How do you add a Blind Carbon Copy field to a message?

9 True or false? An attached image will be displayed inline with the remainder of the email message.

10 If you are sending several large images as attachments, how can you resize the images before sending the message?

11 On which tab is the command to print an email message?

Independent practice activity

In this activity, you'll attach a file to a message, check a message for spelling errors, and save an attached file. You'll also reply to a message and forward a message. You will need to work with a partner to complete this activity.

The files for this activity are in Student Data folder **Unit 2\Unit summary**.

1 Compose a message as shown in Exhibit 2-14. (*Hint:* Enter the name of your mailing partner in the To box and in the message area.)

2 Attach the file **New rules** to the message.

3 Check the message for spelling errors.

4 Send the message to your partner.

5 Read the message you receive from your email partner.

6 Save the attached file with the name **My new rules**.

7 Reply to the email message. In the message area, enter **Thanks for the email. I'll forward a copy to the purchasing team.**

8 Forward the message to another student in the class (someone other than your partner).

9 Close the Message window, if necessary.

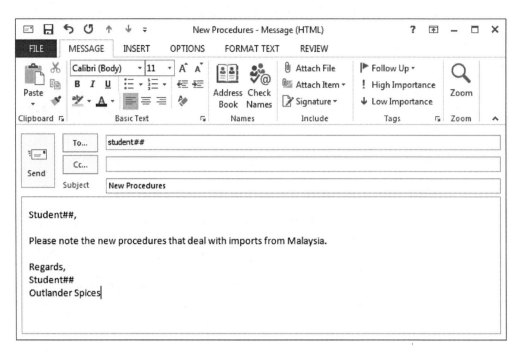

Exhibit 2-14: Independent Practice Activity after step 1

Unit 3

Email management

Complete this unit, and you'll know how to:

A Set message options such as sensitivity and importance, and set up delivery and read-receipt options for messages.

B Organize messages by using views and by sorting and grouping messages.

C Add users to the Blocked Senders and Safe Senders lists, mark messages as Not Junk, and manage junk email options.

Topic A: Setting message options

This topic covers the following Microsoft Office Specialist exam objectives for Outlook 2013.

#	Objective
2.1	**Create a Message**
2.1.9	Prioritize messages
2.1.10	Mark as private
2.1.11	Request delivery/read receipt
2.1.12	Redirect replies
2.3	**Organize and Manage Messages**
2.3.7	Mark as read/unread
2.3.8	Flag messages

Explanation

When you send an email message, you might want the recipient to know whether it's sensitive (personal or confidential) and whether it's urgent so that he or she can respond accordingly.

Setting the sensitivity level

You can specify the sensitivity level for an email message. There are four levels of sensitivity: Normal (default), Personal, Private, and Confidential. When you set the sensitivity to a setting other than Normal, a notice indicating the sensitivity level will appear in the message's InfoBar for the recipient.

To set the sensitivity of a message:

1   Create a message.
2   On the Ribbon, click the Dialog Box Launcher in the Tags group, shown in Exhibit 3-1, to open the message Properties dialog box, shown in Exhibit 3-2.
3   Under Settings, select the Sensitivity level you want to use. You can also select an Importance level by using this dialog box.
4   Click Close.
5   Send the message.

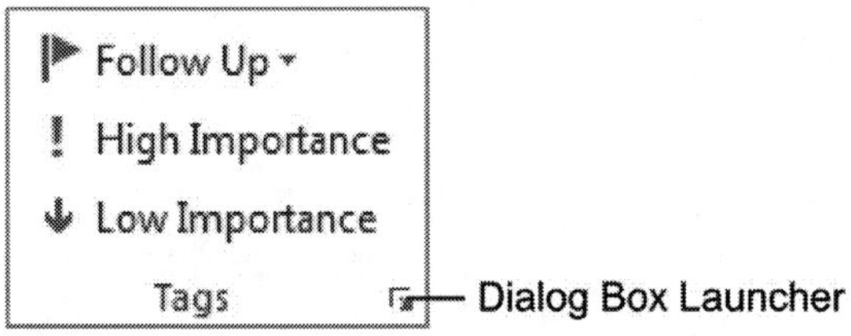

Exhibit 3-1: The Dialog Box Launcher in the Tags group

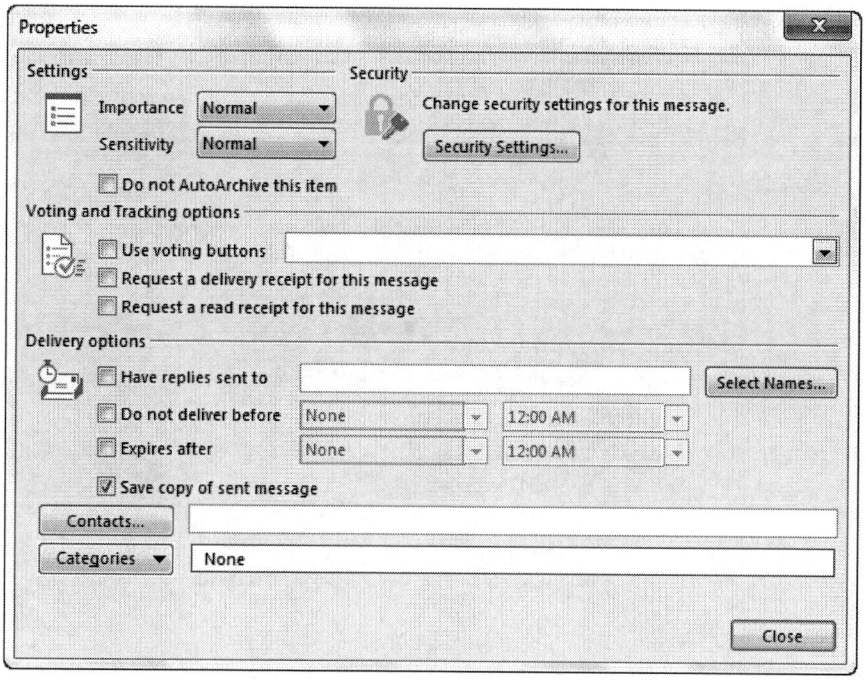

Exhibit 3-2: The message Properties dialog box

Setting the importance level

Use Outlook's importance levels to indicate whether a message is urgent. When you set the importance level for a message to High, a red exclamation mark in the message header tells the recipient that the message needs an immediate response. The default level of importance for a message is Normal. You can also set the importance to Low for messages that don't need a response or that are not a high priority.

To change the importance level for a message, click the High Importance button or the Low Importance button in the Tags group on the Ribbon, as shown in Exhibit 3-1. If neither button is activated, the importance level is set to Normal.

A-1:   Defining delivery options

Here's how	Here's why
1 Open a new Message window	(Click New Email.) You need to know the time of a team meeting. You'll send a message of high importance to your partner.
Address the message to your partner	
In the Subject box, enter **Meeting time?**	
In the message area, type **Help! I forgot the time of today's team meeting.**	
2 In the Tags group, click ❗	(On the Ribbon.) To set the importance level to High.
3 Click the Dialog Box Launcher, as shown	
	⚑ Follow Up ▾ ❗ High Importance ↓ Low Importance Tags
	To open the message's Properties dialog box.
4 Under Settings, from the Sensitivity list, select **Private**	Text in the InfoBar will inform the recipient that this email message is private. He or she will not be able to modify it when forwarding or replying to it.
5 Click **Close**	To close the Properties dialog box.
6 Send the message	
7 Observe your Inbox	Student02 ❗ **Meeting time?** 4:54 PM Help! I forgot the time of today's team
	Your partner's message will be listed in your Inbox after a few moments. The red exclamation point indicates that the message was marked as being important.

8 Select the **Meeting time?** message

Mon 2/11/2013 4:54 PM
Student02
Meeting time?
To   Student01
ℹ️ Please treat this as Private.
This message was sent with High importance.

In the Reading pane, the InfoBar informs you that the message is private.

9 Click **Reply**

You'll send the time of the team meeting. Notice that the High Importance button is not selected. By default, the importance level resets to Normal when you reply to a message.

In the message area, type **The meeting is tomorrow at 10:30 AM.**

Send the reply

The original message is still selected, and its InfoBar now indicates that you replied.

10 Click **Forward**

You'll forward this message to another person. Notice that the High Importance button is selected. The importance level does not reset to Normal when you forward a message.

11 Click **High Importance**

(In the Tags group.) To remove the High Importance level.

12 Send the message to another student

In the To box, enter the address of a student other than your partner. When the forwarded message is received, no exclamation point appears.

Delaying email delivery

Explanation

You can delay the delivery of an email message. When you do so, the message is not sent until the date and time you specify.

To delay the delivery of a message:

1 Create a message.

2 Open the message's Properties dialog box by using either of these techniques:
   - On the Message tab, in the Tags group, click the Dialog Box Launcher. In the dialog box, check "Do not deliver before."
   - On the Options tab, in the More Options group, click Delay Delivery. In the dialog box, "Do not deliver before" is checked automatically.

3 Next to "Do not deliver before," specify the date and time when you want the message to be sent.

4 Click Close.

5 Finish the message and click Send.

A-2:   Specifying a delayed email delivery

Here's how	Here's why
1 Open a new Message window	
Address the message to your partner	
In the Subject box, enter **Reminder**	
2 In the message area, type **Don't forget we have a meeting at 10:30.**	The meeting you're referring to is scheduled for tomorrow, so you'll delay the message so it is sent tomorrow.
3 Click the **Options** tab	
4 In the More Options group, click **Delay Delivery**	To open the Properties dialog box. Under Delivery options, "Do not deliver before" is checked.
5 From the list next to "Do not deliver before," select tomorrow's date	
6 From the time list, select **8:00 AM**	To specify the time at which the email message can be sent.
7 Click **Close**	
8 Click **Send**	To send the message. It won't be received until after 8 AM tomorrow.
9 Observe your Outbox folder	(In the Folder pane.) One message is in your Outbox.
Select **Outbox**	To view your Outbox.
Click the **Send/Receive** tab and then click **Send/Receive All Folders**	One item remains in your Outbox. Your scheduled note will remain there until the delivery time you specified.
10 Select **Inbox**	To view your Inbox again.
Click the **Home** tab	

Specifying email reply addresses

Explanation

By default, when a recipient replies to an email message, the reply is sent to the original sender's address. However, when you send a message, you might want replies to be sent to a different address. For example, if you use more than one email account, you might send a message from one account but want replies to go to another account. Alternately, you might want a response to go to a colleague.

To specify an email address to which replies are sent:

1 Create a message.

2 Open the message's Properties dialog box:

- On the Message tab, in the Tags group, click the Dialog Box Launcher. In the dialog box, check "Have replies sent to."

- On the Options tab, in the More Options group, click Direct Replies To. In the dialog box, "Have replies sent to" is checked automatically.

3 Next to "Have replies sent to," specify the email address to which you want replies sent.

4 Click Close.

5 Finish the message and click Send.

Do it!

A-3:   Specifying an email reply address

Here's how	Here's why
1 Open a new Message window Address the message to your partner In the Subject box, enter **Out Thursday**	
2 In the message area, type **I'll be out of town Thursday. Contact me in an emergency.**	You'll specify your personal email address for any replies to this message, because while you're out of town, you'll be checking your personal email.
3 Click the **Options** tab	
4 Click **Direct Replies To**	(In the More Options group.) To open the Properties dialog box. Under Delivery options, "Have replies sent to" is checked.
5 Next to "Have replies sent to," enter an alternate email address	Specify an alternate email address provided by your instructor. If no alternate is available, just enter your assigned email address.
6 Click **Close**	
7 Click **Send**	

Requesting read and delivery receipts

Sometimes it's important to know when a message is delivered to the recipient and when each recipient reads the message. You can track when the messages you sent are delivered and when they are read.

To request notification when a message has been delivered, check "Request a Delivery Receipt" in the Tracking group on the Options tab. When the message is delivered to the user's Inbox, you will receive a message stating that delivery was successful.

To request notification when the message has been read by each recipient, check "Request a Read Receipt" in the Tracking group on the Options tab. When the recipient opens the message, he or she is notified that you've requested a read receipt. The recipient has the option of sending or denying a read receipt. You can identify notification messages in your Inbox by the word "Read:" before the subject.

A-4: Using delivery and read receipts

Here's how	Here's why
1 Create a message and address it to your partner	
Enter the subject **Cinnamon prices in Malaysia**	
In the message area, type **Cinnamon prices doubled today. We'll need to revise our prices.**	
2 Click the **Options** tab	
In the Tracking group, check **Request a Delivery Receipt**	You'll receive a return message with the date and time the message was delivered to the recipient's Inbox.
In the Tracking group, check **Request a Read Receipt**	You'll receive a return message with the date and time when the recipient opens the message.
3 Send the message to your partner	
4 Observe your Inbox	Microsoft Outlook ⊗☲ Delivered: Cinnamon prices in Mala... 9:41 AM Your message has been delivered to
	The icon above the time indicates that your message was received by your partner. This is your delivery receipt message.
Select the delivery receipt message	(The one with the icon.) In the Reading pane, you'll see a message stating that your email was delivered and listing the recipients.

5 Double-click the **Cinnamon Prices in Malaysia** message	(The message your partner sent you.) To open it. You're prompted to send a read receipt to your partner. (You will not be prompted if you preview the message.)
Click **Yes**	To send the read receipt message.
6 Close the Message window	
7 Observe the read receipt message	Student02 ⌾ᶟ Read: Cinnamon prices in Malaysia 9:50 AM Your message The message with Read: in the subject line is the read receipt. Notice the checkmark icon.
Select the read receipt	In the Reading pane, the message states when your message was read.

Message flags

Explanation

When you receive an email message that you need to follow up on, you can flag it as a reminder. You can also send a flagged message to other people. The message will then alert the recipients that immediate action is needed for that message. Flagged messages create to-do items either for you alone or for you and the recipients of the message.

If your Inbox contains many email messages, you might think it will be difficult to search for flagged messages. However, flagged messages are displayed in the Task list, as shown in Exhibit 3-3.

Arrange by: Flag: Due Date | Today   ▲
Type a new task
▲ ⚑ Today
Cinnamon prices in Malaysia   ☐ ⚑

Exhibit 3-3: Flagged messages in the Task list

Sending a flag and reminder with a new message

You can flag a new message and create a reminder for message recipients by using the Follow Up button in the Tags group on the Ribbon. Just click Follow Up and choose Add Reminder. By default, the message will be flagged for you, and a reminder will be created for a time in the future. Use the Custom dialog box, shown in Exhibit 3-4, to change the reminder time to a time that is appropriate for you.

To flag a message for recipients and create a reminder for them, check Flag for Recipients and specify the date and time you want the reminder to be displayed.

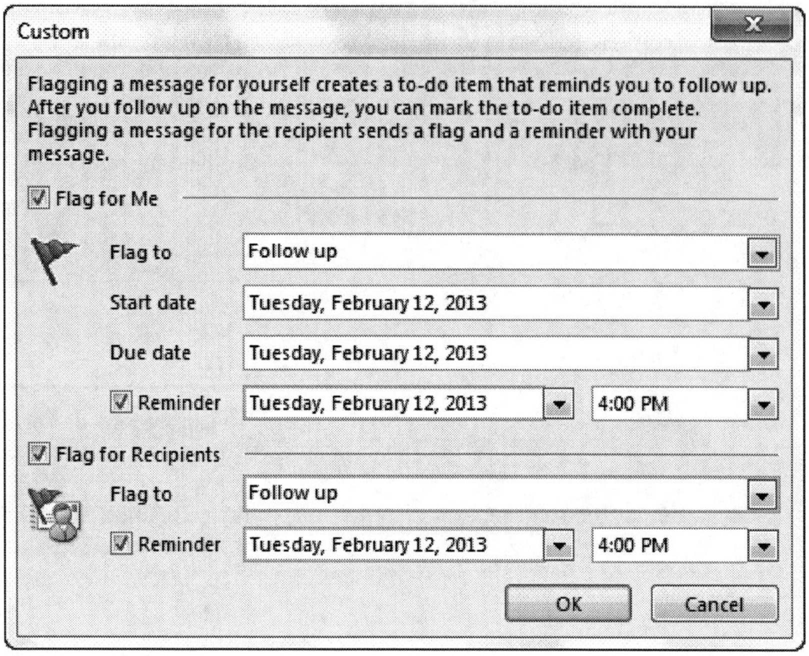

Exhibit 3-4: Creating reminders

Flagging received messages

Flagging a message identifies it for further action by inserting a flag symbol on the right side of it in the Message list. When you flag a received message, you can specify the action to be taken, the due date, and the time.

To flag a message, right-click the flag column to the right of the message and choose one of the menu options shown in Exhibit 3-5. After you set the flag, the InfoBar displays the option you chose. Your flagged message will appear in the To-Do list, in Tasks, and in the Daily Task list in the Calendar.

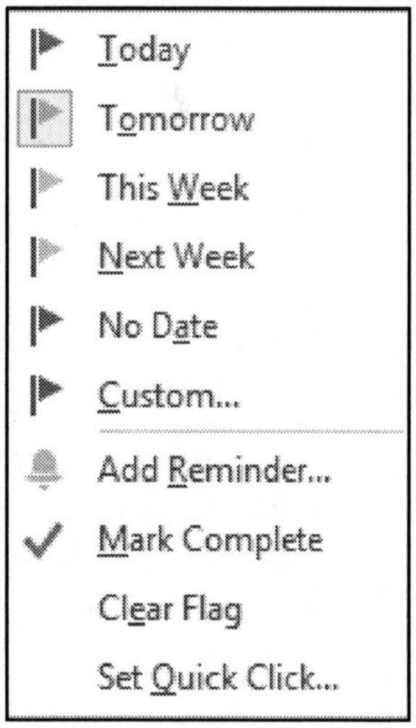

Exhibit 3-5: The Flag menu

Marking a flagged message as completed

After you follow up on a flagged message, you can mark it as completed. You can work with flagged messages in either the Tasks list or the Message list. To mark a flagged item as complete, right-click the message and choose Mark Complete. The flag changes to a checkmark, and the message is removed from the Task list.

Clearing a message flag

If you want to remove the flag from an email message, choose Clear Flag from the Flag menu. When you clear a flag, there is no record of the message ever appearing in views such as Tasks. If you want to keep a record of completed items, use the Mark Complete option.

Marking a message as read and unread

Unread messages are shown in dark blue text in the Message list. When you select a message from the Message list, it is automatically marked as read and appears in the Reading pane. To mark a message as unread, right-click it from the Message list and choose the Mark as Unread option.

Do it!

A-5: Flagging an email message

Here's how	Here's why
1 Select the **Cinnamon prices in Malaysia** message	Make sure you select the message sent to you by your partner.
2 Click the flag icon	Student02 ⚑ Cinnamon prices in Malaysia 9:49 AM Cinnamon prices doubled today. We'll
	(Move the mouse pointer over the message to show the Flag icon.) To flag the message for follow-up. The message now has a red flag and appears under Today in the Tasks list. By default, flagged messages are flagged under Today.
Observe the Reading pane	The InfoBar lists start-by and due-by dates. The default flag marks items as due today.
3 Right-click the flag for the "Cinnamon prices in Malaysia" message	
Choose **Next Week**	
Observe the Reading pane	The InfoBar now indicates that you must follow up by the Friday of next week.

4 Right-click the flag for the
"Cinnamon prices in Malaysia"
message

   Choose **Mark Complete**   The icon becomes a checkmark.

   Observe the Reading pane   The InfoBar now indicates that you have
completed this task.

5 Right-click the checkmark for the
"Cinnamon prices in Malaysia"
message

   Choose **Clear Flag**   To remove the flag from the message. The
InfoBar message is also removed.

6 Create a message to your partner,
with the subject **Price updates**

7 In the message area, type
**Call me today to talk
about price changes.**

8 Click **Follow Up** and choose
Add Reminder...   To open the Custom dialog box, shown in
Exhibit 3-4.

9 Check **Flag for Recipients**,
and check **Reminder**

   Choose today's date, and set the   (Select the numbers in the Time box.) For
reminder time for 10 minutes from   example, if it's 1:17 p.m., change the time for
the current time   the reminder to 1:27 p.m.

   Click **OK**   To close the Custom dialog box.

10 Observe the top of the message   (Below the Ribbon.) Your reminder and your
recipient's reminder information is displayed.

   Send the message

11 Select the new message in your
Inbox

> **Student02**   🔔 👤▶
> Price updates   11:02 AM
> Call me today to talk about price

The message has been flagged, and a reminder
(indicated by the bell icon) has been created.

   Deselect the message   By selecting any other message. The message is
not read until you select something else.

12 Right-click the message and select   This is helpful when you quickly glance at a
Mark as Unread   message, but need to return to it later to actually
read it.

The Reminders window

Explanation

The Reminders window is like an alarm clock. It will open on the date and at the time specified in any reminders you have created or have been sent in Outlook. You can use the options in the Reminders window, shown in Exhibit 3-6, to see details about the reminder or to dismiss the reminder. You can also set a snooze function to have the Reminders window open again, anywhere from 5 minutes to 2 weeks in the future.

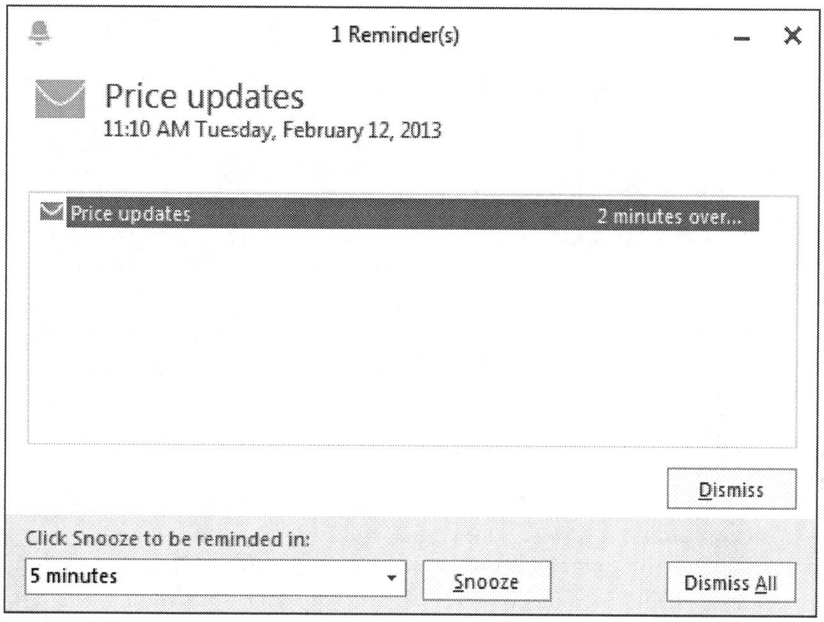

Exhibit 3-6: The Reminders window

Do it!

A-6: Using the Reminders window

Here's how	Here's why
1 Wait for the Reminders window to open	(If necessary.) You'll see the Price updates message that your partner sent to you.
2 Right-click the reminder and click **Open** Close the message	To open the message for which the reminder was set.
3 In the Reminders window, verify that the reminder item is selected, and click **Dismiss**	To remove the reminder.

Topic B: Organizing the Inbox folder

This topic covers the following Microsoft Office Specialist exam objectives for Outlook 2013.

#	Objective
1.1	**Customize Outlook Settings**
1.1.5	Configure views
1.4	**Search in Outlook**
1.4.2	Search for messages
2.3	**Organize and Manage Messages**
2.3.1	Sort messages

Explanation

Outlook provides you with various tools and techniques for organizing your Inbox, including views and folders. You can also sort and arrange messages.

Working with views

A view is a set of options for displaying messages or items in a folder. For example, in the Inbox's Compact view, messages are listed in reverse chronological order. The sender is displayed on one line. The Subjects are displayed with the date on a second line. The third line shows the beginning text of the message contents and can be customized to show up to three lines of text or no lines. The Reading pane displays the entire contents of the selected message.

Outlook includes several built-in views, each of which you can customize. You can also create your own custom views. A view is made up of a view type, fields, grouping and sorting options, colors, and fonts.

Changing the view

To change the view, click the View tab. Then click Change View and choose the view you want to use. The Change View menu is shown in Exhibit 3-7.

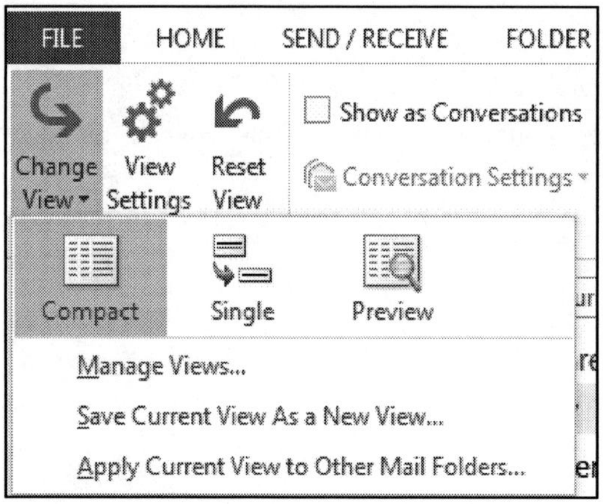

Exhibit 3-7: Changing the view in the Inbox folder

Do it!   **B-1:   Changing views**

Here's how	Here's why
1 Display your Inbox	(In the Folder pane, click Mail and select Inbox.) The current view displays all messages in the Inbox in a three-line format.
2 Click the **View** tab	
Click **Change View** and choose **Single**	To switch to the Single view. Messages are now shown in a two-line format.
Click where indicated	 SUBJECT RE... | S. Sort by: Subject Price updates Tu... 9. You can sort the messages by clicking a column's header.
3 Change to the **Preview** view	(Click Change View and choose Preview.) The Reading pane is hidden, and messages are listed in a two-line format that spans the width formerly shared by the Message list and Reading pane.
4 Change to the **Compact** view	To return to the default Inbox view.
5 From the View menu, click **Message Preview**	
Choose **3 Lines**	To show three lines of text for the message contents for each email in the Message list. A message displays asking if you want to change the preview setting in All mailboxes, or only This folder.
Click **This Folder**	Notice the emails in the Message list show up to three lines of message text.
6 Change the Message list to show only one line of message text	Click Message Preview and choose 1 Line.

Arranging, sorting, and filtering items

Explanation   You can arrange the items in your Message list based on various criteria, such as the date, the sender's name, or the subject. You can also sort the items in ascending or descending order. By default, messages in the Inbox are grouped by date. The newest messages appear at the top of the Folder Message list.

You can choose one of the predefined arrangements described in the following table or create a custom arrangement. Unless otherwise specified, in all of the arrangements, messages are sorted by date, with the newest messages listed first.

Arrangement	Grouped by...
Date	Date sent.
From	Sender.
To	First recipient in the To line.
Categories	Categories, with uncategorized messages listed first, followed by categories in alphabetical order.
Flag: Start Date	Flagged messages by start date. (No Date items are listed first, followed by groups for any other specified start dates.)
Flag: Due Date	Flagged messages by due date. (No Date items are listed first, followed by groups for any other specified due dates.)
Size	Message size in the following categories: Enormous (> 5 MB), Huge (1–5 MB), Very Large (500 KB–1 MB), Large (100–500 KB), Medium (25–100 KB), Small (10–25 KB), and Tiny (< 10 KB).
Subject	Subject, alphabetically.
Type	Item type, such as Message (email messages), Automatic Reply, Meeting request, and so forth.
Attachments	Messages with attachments and those without attachments.
Account	Email accounts defined on your system.
Importance	Importance level (High, Normal, and Low), with the highest-priority messages listed first (at the top).

Selecting an arrangement

Outlook provides at least three means to set the arrangement of messages in the Message list. These are:

- Click the View tab and then click the desired arrangement type in the Arrangement group.
- Right-click the heading of the Message list, choose an arrangement type.

Sorting an arrangement

Each of the arrangements has a default sorting order for its groupings. For example, the Importance arrangement lists the most important messages at the top. Within a group, messages are listed in chronological order, with the newest messages listed first.

You can change the grouping order with a simple click. Notice the label of the Header changes, depending on the arrangement you have selected. For example, with messages arranged by Conversations, you'll see the label "Newest" in the header of the Message list. With the Importance arrangement active, that same header is labeled "High" Regardless of its label, click that button to reverse the sorting order.

Ungrouping messages

By default, items are arranged in groups. For example, arranging items by Importance creates a view in which messages with the same Importance level are listed together, along with a heading. You can display messages without this grouping. In that case, messages are simply listed, one after the other, in the Message list, ordered by the criteria you selected for the arrangement and sorting.

To display messages without the grouping, click the Arrange By button in the Arrangement group on the View tab. Then choose Show in Groups to clear the option.

Filtering unread emails

By default, all messages are shown in the Message list. If you are looking for a specific unread message, you can use the Unread button at the top of the Message list to apply a filter that only displays unread emails. To return to viewing all email messages, use the All button in the Message list.

Do it!

B-2:   Arranging, sorting, and filtering messages

Here's how	Here's why
1 Click the **View** tab	If necessary.
2 In the Arrangement group, click **Arrange By**	
3 Choose **Importance**	To arrange messages by importance.
4 Arrange the Message list by Size	Click Arrange By and choose Size.
Choose **Size**	To arrange messages in groups by size.
5 Click **Largest**	
	To change the sorting order—in this case, to smallest first.
6 Click **Calendar**	From the Navigation bar.
Click **Mail**	The arrangement and sorting of messages is preserved as you switch between folders.
7 Click the **Arrange By** button	
Click **Show in Groups**	To clear the option and show messages without grouping them. Messages are still arranged by size and sorted from smallest to largest. However, the groupings and headings are no longer displayed.
8 Click **Reset View**	
Click **Yes**	To reset the view to its default settings: Arrange by Date with Newest on Top.
9 Click **Unread**	
	At the top of the Message list. The Message list shows a filtered view of the Inbox with only the Unread messages displayed.
Click **All**	To remove the Unread filter and show all emails in the Inbox.

Outlook search tools

You will probably find it more and more difficult to find the information you need as your Inbox grows and you amass a collection of folders, messages, and other items. Fortunately, Outlook provides search tools you can use to sift through the clutter to find just the items you need.

Instant Search

The *Instant Search* feature, available in the Message list, enables you to quickly search the current folder. For example, as shown in Exhibit 3-8, when you're viewing your Inbox folder, Instant Search provides a way to search your Inbox for messages. By default, Instant Search does not look in subfolders. But if the results don't include what you're looking for, you can expand your search to include subfolders.

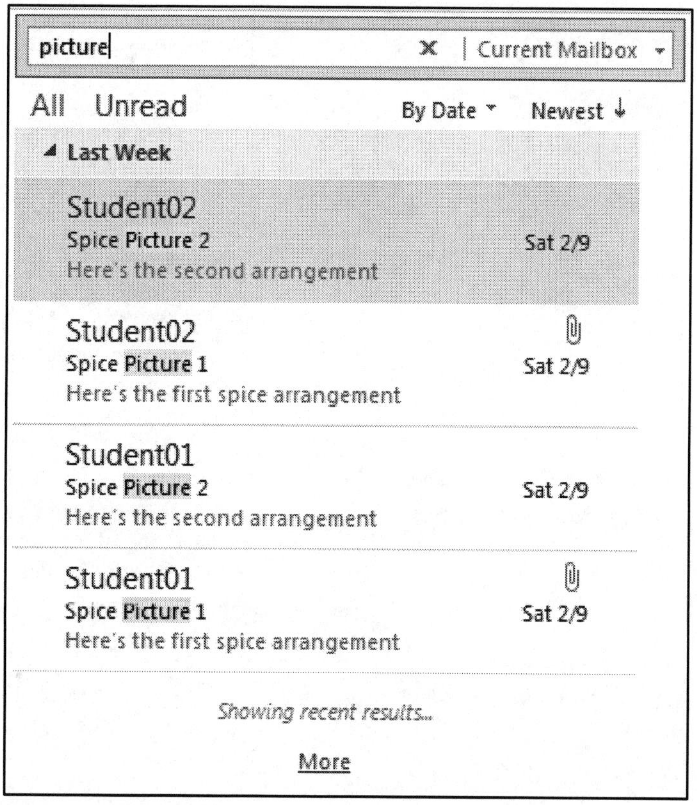

Exhibit 3-8: Instant Search with search results

After typing the search text, messages that contain the text are shown in the Message list. Each instance of the search text is highlighted in the messages displayed.

Do it!

B-3: Using Instant Search

Here's how	Here's why
1 In the Search field, enter **Price**	

price   ✕   Current Mailbox ▾
All   Unread   By Date ▾   Newest ↓
◢ Yesterday
Student02
Price updates   Tue 11:02 AM
Call me today to talk about price
Student01   🔔 📭 🏳
Price updates   Tue 11:00 AM
Call me today to talk about price
Student02   ◉⥱
Read: Cinnamon prices in Malaysia   Tue 9:50 AM
Your message
Student02   ✓
Cinnamon prices in Malaysia   Tue 9:49 AM
Cinnamon prices doubled today. We'll
Microsoft Outlook   ◉⥱
Delivered: Cinnamon prices in Malay...   Tue 9:41 AM
Your message has been delivered to
Student01   ⁝⁝
Cinnamon prices in Malaysia   Tue 9:40 AM
Cinnamon prices doubled today. We'll

To search for messages containing the word "Price." Your results might not match the image shown here exactly, but they should include the "Price updates" and "Cinnamon prices in Malaysia" messages.

Notice that Outlook searched the Current Mailbox by default

Messages that you received in your Inbox and messages from your Sent Items folder appear in the Message list. You can also specify to search just the Current Folder, Subfolders or All Outlook Items.

From the Instant Search box, select **Current Folder**

Current Mailbox ▾
Current Folder 🖱
Subfolders
Current Mailbox
All Outlook Items

To only show Inbox messages.

2 Add **Cinnamon** before the word Price in the Search field

To narrow the search in the Message list. Now only the messages from the Cinnamon prices in Malaysia thread are shown.

3 Click as shown

✕🖱   Cu
By Date ▾

To clear the search results and return to the Inbox folder.

Topic C: Managing junk email

This topic covers the following Microsoft Office Specialist exam objectives for Outlook 2013.

#	Objective
1.0	**Customize Outlook Settings**
1.1.4	Block specific addresses
2.3	**Organize and Manage Messages**
2.3.5	Configure junk e-mail settings

Explanation

You might get unwanted or junk email messages, which can clog your Inbox if they're not managed properly. *Junk email messages* include unsolicited business promotion messages, advertisements, or messages with adult content. Outlook provides various tools to help you manage such messages. These tools include:

- The Junk Email folder
- The Junk Email Filter
- The Blocked Senders list
- The Safe Senders list
- Additional options

The Junk Email folder

Messages that Outlook determines to be junk are stored in a folder named Junk Email. It is a good idea to review the messages in this folder from time to time to make sure they are not legitimate messages that you want to see.

If messages in your Junk Email folder are legitimate, you can move them back to the Inbox. You can right-click the message and choose Junk, Not Junk, or you can simply drag the message to your Inbox (or any other folder). After you review the messages in your Junk Email folder, you can empty the folder.

You can configure Outlook to automatically delete the messages it determines to be junk. If you do so, messages will not be moved to the Junk Email folder. You will not have an opportunity to rescue misidentified, legitimate messages before they're deleted.

The Junk Email filter

Outlook examines the messages you receive to determine if they are legitimate or junk. It uses the rules defined in the Junk Email filter to make this determination. Your Exchange administrator can manage the rules associated with that filter. Users can set a sensitivity level:

- **No Automatic Filtering** — Junk email filtering is disabled and all messages are delivered to your Inbox. You will have to manually manage junk email if you use this option.

- **Low** — This default option is designed to catch the most obvious junk email messages while catching the fewest legitimate messages.

- **High** — Most junk email messages are caught, but a higher percentage of legitimate messages are misidentified as junk.

- **Safe Senders Lists Only** — Messages from anyone not on your Safe Senders or Safe Recipients lists will be marked as junk.

The Blocked Senders list

You can block messages from a sender by adding the sender's email address or domain name to the Blocked Senders list. When you do this, Outlook places any future messages from that sender in the Junk Email folder. (In an Exchange environment, you cannot block senders within your own organization.)

There are at least three ways to add a sender to the Blocked Senders list:

- In the Message list, right-click a message from that sender and choose Junk, Block Sender.

- With a message from the sender open, click the Junk button in the Delete group on the Message tab and choose Block Sender.

- Click Junk and choose Junk Email Options to open the Junk Email Options dialog box. Click the Blocked Senders tab. Click Add, enter the offending address, and click OK.

The Safe Senders list

Messages from senders on your Safe Senders list are never treated as junk. In an Exchange environment, you cannot add senders in your own organization to your Safe Senders list, but they are treated as if they were on that list.

There are at least three ways to add a sender to the Safe Senders list:

- In the Message list, right-click a message from that sender and choose Junk, Never Block Sender.

- With a message from the sender open, click the Junk button in the Delete group on the Message tab and choose Never Block Sender.

- Click Junk and choose Junk Email Options to open the Junk Email Options dialog box. Click the Safe Senders tab. Click Add, enter the email address, and click OK.

Additional options

Outlook includes additional features for managing junk email. They are described in the following table.

Feature	Description
Safe Recipients list	Email sent to addresses on this list will never be treated as junk. Use this option to prevent mail addressed to email lists and groups to which you belong from being treated as junk.
Postmarking	By default, Outlook stamps each outgoing message with a digital postmark. You could configure Outlook to treat messages that arrive without a postmark as junk. However, only Outlook supports this feature, so you would block potentially legitimate messages from senders using other email applications.
Auto Picture Download	Senders of bulk junk email use Web beacons to determine which addresses are legitimate and which are invalid. A *Web beacon* is a special type of image or file embedded in an email message. When you view the image, a signal is sent to the sender, notifying him or her of your email address. For this reason, by default, Outlook does not display pictures from Internet senders (those outside your organization).
International options	You can configure Outlook to automatically block mail from international domains. For example, many email scams have originated in Nigeria. To block such messages, you could block all messages from the .ng domain. However, mailers of junk messages frequently falsify sender addresses, making domain-wide blocking a less than perfect way to filter junk email.

Do it!

C-1: Exploring junk email management features

Here's how	Here's why
1 Right-click a message from your partner	It does not matter which message.
Point to **Junk**	Block Sender Never Block Sender Never Block Sender's Domain (@example.com) Never Block this Group or Mailing List Not Junk Junk E-mail Options...
	To display the Junk Email menu. You could use the commands on this menu to add the sender to your Blocked Senders or Safe Senders lists.
2 Press ESC twice	To close the menus.

3	On the Home tab, in the Delete group, click **Junk**	To display the same menu.
	Choose **Junk Email Options...**	To open the Junk Email Options dialog box.
4	Observe the four levels for handling junk email	

> Choose the level of junk e-mail protection you want:
>
> ⦿ No Automatic Filtering. Mail from blocked senders is still moved to the Junk E-mail folder.
>
> ○ Low: Move the most obvious junk e-mail to the Junk E-mail folder.
>
> ○ High: Most junk e-mail is caught, but some regular mail may be caught as well. Check your Junk E-mail folder often.
>
> ○ Safe Lists Only: Only mail from people or domains on your Safe Senders List or Safe Recipients List will be delivered to your Inbox.

		You could choose another protection level, but the default is suitable in most cases.
	Observe the option to delete suspected junk email	This setting deletes junk email rather than storing it in your Junk Email folder. You should probably not use this setting. Otherwise, you could miss legitimate email that has been misidentified as junk.
5	Click the **Safe Senders** tab	Add senders to this list to be sure that mail from them is never considered to be junk.
6	Click the **Safe Recipients** tab	Add senders to this list so that mail addressed to them is not considered to be junk. Use this option for email lists and groups you belong to.
7	Click the **Blocked Senders** tab	Add senders to this list to be sure that mail from them is always considered to be junk.
8	Click the **International** tab	Use the options here to manage the junk email handling for messages from other countries.
9	Click **Cancel**	To close the dialog box without changing settings.

Unit summary: Email management

Topic A   In this topic, you learned how to set **importance** and **sensitivity levels** for messages. You also specified a **delayed delivery** for a message and specified an alternate address for email replies. Then, you learned how to **flag messages** and mark flagged messages as completed. You also learned how to request a **read receipt** and use the **Reminders** window.

Topic B   In this topic, you organized the messages in your Inbox. You learned how to change or customize the default Inbox view. You also **arranged** and **sorted** messages.

Topic C   In this topic, you learned how to manage **junk email**. You learned how to add senders to the Blocked Senders list and add senders and domains to the Safe Senders List. Then you learned how to mark a message as Not Junk and empty the Junk Email folder. You also learned how to change the **junk email level** and configure other options for handling junk email.

Independent practice activity

In this activity, you'll specify a read receipt and an importance level for a new message. You'll flag a message, reply to a flagged message, and change your junk email settings. You'll also add a sender to your Safe Senders list.

1 Compose a message with the text, **I forgot the date for the project-planning meeting. Can you please remind me?** Address the message to your partner.

2 Specify the subject as **Forgot**.

3 Set the options so that you receive a read receipt.

4 Set the importance level to High.

5 Send the message.

6 Read the message from your partner. When prompted, send a receipt.

7 Open the read receipt and read it. (*Hint:* Activate the Inbox.)

8 Close the Message window.

9 Create a flagged message to reply by 4:30 PM today, and send it to your partner. Enter any subject and message text. (*Hint:* In the Tags group on the Message tab, click Follow Up and choose Add Reminder. Check Flag for Recipients.)

10 Reply to the flagged message and mark it as completed.

11 Change the junk email level to High. (*Hint:* Use the Junk Email Options dialog box.)

12 Add **samwilkens@doverspiceworks.com** to your Safe Senders list.

13 Arrange the messages in the Inbox folder based on their size. Change the sort order to show the messages from the smallest to the largest.

14 Restore the default sort order for your Inbox.

Review questions

1 On the Message tab, which group contains the buttons for setting the importance of a message?

   A Send

   B Tags

   C Options

   D Editing

2 What is the advantage of marking a message as private?

3 What does a red exclamation mark indicate?

4 How can you block messages from an entire domain?

5 True or false? You should just delete all messages in your Junk Email folder without reviewing them.

6 What should you do if a legitimate message ends up in your Junk Email folder?

Unit 4

Contacts

Complete this unit, and you'll know how to:

A Use the Contacts folder to add, modify, organize, and print business and personal contacts.

B View address books and import contact data from Excel.

C Create and modify a contact group.

Topic A: Working with contacts

This topic covers the following Microsoft Office Specialist exam objectives for Outlook 2013.

#	Objective
1.3	**Print and Save Information in Outlook**
1.3.5	Print contacts
4.1	**Create and Manage Contacts**
4.1.1	Create new contacts
4.1.2	Delete contacts
4.1.4	Edit contact information
4.1.5	Attach an image to contacts
4.1.6	Add tags to contacts
3.4	**Create and Manage Notes, Tasks, and Journals**
3.4.3	Attach notes to contacts

Explanation

A *contact* is a person with whom you have either a business or personal relationship. You use the Contacts folder to manage information about each contact, such as the person's name, address, telephone number, email address, Web site address, company name, birthday, and anniversary. Contacts are integrated with the Inbox and the Calendar for sending email and scheduling meetings. For example, when you enter a contact's birthday, it's automatically entered in the Calendar.

You can view Contacts by clicking People in the Navigation bar.

Adding a contact

Explanation

There are various ways you can add a contact to your Contacts list. You can use the new Contact window, or add a contact from the header of a received email message.

To add a contact by using the new Contact window:

1 Click People in the Navigation bar.
2 Click New Contact to open a new Contact window, as shown in Exhibit 4-1.
3 Enter information about the contact, such as the person's name, address, telephone number, and fax number.
4 In the Actions group, click Save & Close.

To add a contact from a received email message:

1 Open or preview the message in the Reading pane.
2 In the message header, right-click the sender's email address and choose Add to Outlook Contacts from the shortcut menu.
3 In the Contact Card window, enter any additional information needed.
4 Click Save & Close.

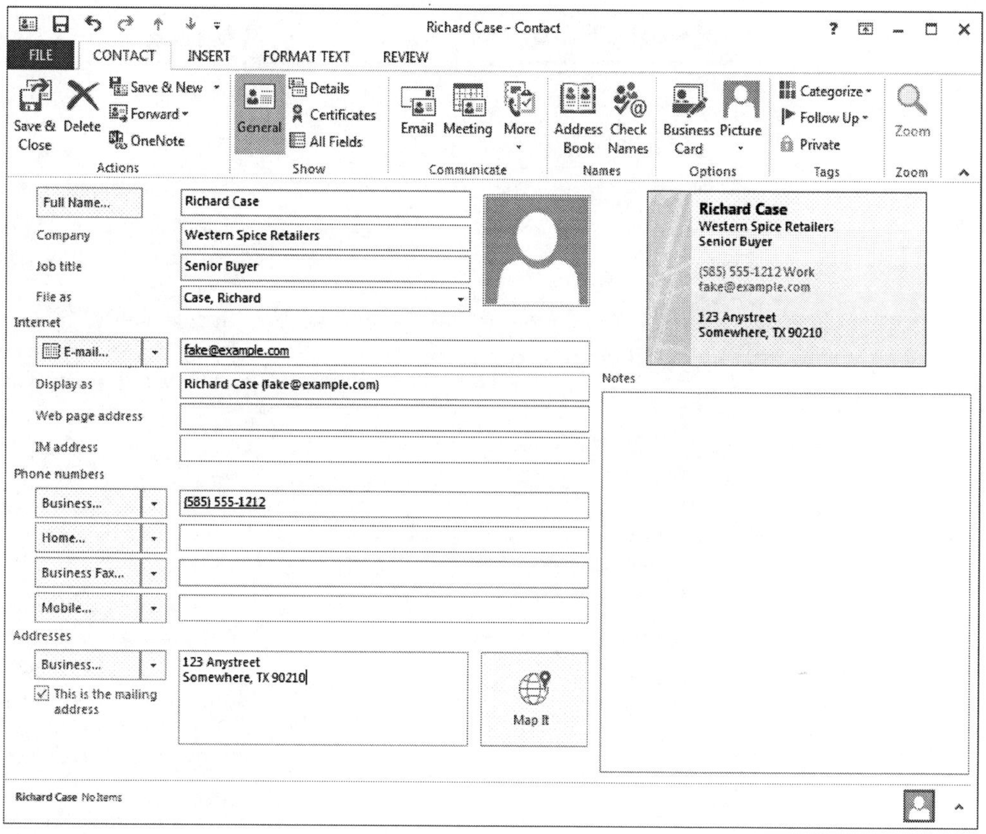

Exhibit 4-1: A sample Contact window

Exhibit 4-2: Sample Contact Card window

A-1:   Exploring and adding contacts

Here's how	Here's why
1 In the Navigation pane, click **Contacts**	By default, the Contacts folder is empty.
2 Observe the Ribbon	Commands on the Home tab give you access to the most common functions you will use to manage your contacts.
3 Observe the buttons in the middle of the People list	When you click any letter, the contact names beginning with the selected letter appear in the People list, if the list is not empty.
4 Click **New Contact**	(In the New group on the Home tab.) To open a new Contact window.
5 In the Full Name box, enter **Richard Case**	To specify the name of the contact.
Press TAB	To move the insertion point to the next box. The contact's name automatically appears in the format "last name, first name" in the File as list. This setting controls how Outlook saves contact information (alphabetically by last name).
6 In the Company box, enter **Western Spice Retailers**	To specify the contact's company name. This company is a customer of Outlander Spices.
Press TAB	To move the insertion point to the next box.
7 In the Job title box, enter **Senior Buyer**	To specify the contact's job title.
8 In the Email address box, enter **fake@example.com**	
Press TAB	Outlook creates the "Display as" text, using the contact's name and email address.
9 Observe the text boxes under Phone numbers	 There are four boxes for phone numbers: Business, Home, Business Fax, and Mobile.
In the Business number box, enter **(585) 555-1212** and press TAB	 You can enter numbers in various formats, including (585) 555-1212, 585.555.1212, and 585-555-1212.

10 In the Addresses section, enter the address as shown

Addresses

Business...   123 Anystreet
Somewhere, TX 90210
☑ This is the mailing address

Outlook automatically checks "This is the mailing address."

11 On the Contact tab, in the Show group, click **Details**

Here, you can enter details such as the contact's manager, department, birthday, and anniversary.

In the Department box, enter **Marketing**

On the Contact tab, click **General**

(In the Show group.) To return to the general view.

12 In the Actions group, click **Save & Close**

(On the Contact tab.) To save the contact information and close the Contact window.

13 Display your Inbox

Click Mail on the Navigation bar.

14 Select a message from your partner

In the Reading pane, right-click your partner's email address

Choose **Add to Outlook Contacts**

To open a new Contact Card window, displaying your partner's contact information.

If your partner is willing to share his or her full name, enter it in the Name box

You can enter a fictitious name otherwise.

Click **Save**

The Check Full Name window displays.

Click **OK**

Click **Save**

To save the contact.

15 In the Reading pane, point to your partner's email address

Sally Sample

A pop-up is displayed, showing brief information about the contact.

Modifying and deleting contacts

Explanation

After creating a contact item, you might need to change the information. For example, if your client's address changes, you'll need to update the address accordingly. You can modify a contact and then save the changes as the current contact or as a new contact. You can also add various items—such as important documents, business cards, or messages—to your contacts.

To edit a contact, click it from the Contacts list to show the contact information in the People pane as shown in Exhibit 4-3. Then edit the information and save the contact. This saves the changes in the current contact file.

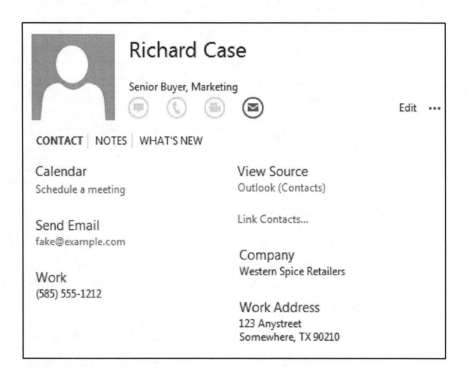

Richard Case

Senior Buyer, Marketing

Edit •••

CONTACT | NOTES | WHAT'S NEW

Calendar
Schedule a meeting

View Source
Outlook (Contacts)

Link Contacts...

Send Email
fake@example.com

Company
Western Spice Retailers

Work
(585) 555-1212

Work Address
123 Anystreet
Somewhere, TX 90210

Exhibit 4-3: The People Pane

Adding an image to contacts

Explanation

You can use a custom photo for your contacts in the People list. To add a photo, select a contact from the People list. Click the Outlook (Contacts) link from the People Pane to display the Contact window. Click the Add Contact Picture button, navigate to the location of the photo and select it, and click Open. The selected photo is shown on the Contact window. Click the Save & Close button to update the contact.

Deleting contacts

Explanation

Over time, you may develop a large quantity of contacts, some of which are no longer needed. If you find that a contact is no longer needed, you can delete it. To delete a contact, select it from the People list and click the Delete button. Any personalized information you added for the contact is deleted.

Do it!

A-2:   Modifying and deleting a contact

The files for this activity are in Student Data folder **Unit 4\Topic A**.

Here's how	Here's why
1 Activate Contacts	From the Navigation bar.
2 Click **Richard Case**	(If necessary.) To show the contact information for Richard Case. You need to change the job title and add a picture for this contact.
3 Click the **Outlook (Contacts)** link	View Source Outlook (Contacts) To open the Contact window for editing.
4 Edit the Job title box to read **Vice President**	
5 Click as shown	
6 Navigate to the current topic folder	Student Data folder Unit 4\Topic A.
Select **man1** and click **OK**	To add the picture to this contact.
7 Observe the business card preview	**Richard Case** Western Spice Retailers Vice President Marketing (585) 555-1212 Work fake@example.com 123 Anystreet Somewhere, TX 90210 The preview reflects your changes.
8 Click **Save & Close**	
9 From the People list, click your partner's contact name	(Or the fictitious name you entered.) You'll delete this contact.
Click the Delete button	X Delete From the Delete group on the Home tab. The contact is deleted from the People list.

Attaching items to contacts

Explanation

You can attach files and Outlook items to a contact. To attach a file, such as a Word document or Excel worksheet, open the contact. Click the Insert tab and click the Attach File button in the Include group. Select the file you want to attach and click Insert. The link to the file will appear in the Notes section. You can view the file by double-clicking its icon.

You can also attach Outlook items, such as a message, another contact, or an appointment, to a contact. Here's how:

1 Open the Contact.
2 Click the Insert tab and click the Outlook Item button in the Include group.
3 From the Look in list, select the folder containing the item.
4 Select the desired item in the Items list and click OK.

Do it!

A-3: Attaching items to a contact

Here's how	Here's why
1 Open the **Richard Case** contact	(Click the contact name and select the Outlook (Contacts) link. You'll attach a Word document to the contact.
2 Click the **Insert** tab	
3 Click [Attach File]	To open the Insert File dialog box.
Navigate to the current topic folder	
Select **Richard Case Bio**	
Click **Insert**	Notes Richard Case Bio.docx An icon for the attached Word document appears in the Notes section.
4 Click the **Contact** tab	
Click **Save & Close**	

Adding tags to contacts

Explanation

There are several ways that you can tag contacts, similar to how you tag email messages. For example, you can tag a contact for follow-up by selecting the contact and clicking the Follow Up button in the Tags group on the Home tab. From the Follow Up list that pops up, select when you want to follow-up. The flagged contact appears on the To Do and Tasks list.

You can also mark a contact as private, so that other people cannot see the details of this contact. To do so, select the contact you wish to make private and click the Private button in the Tags group on the Home tab.

Adding contacts from the same company

Explanation

Several of your contacts might work for the same company. For these contacts, most of the information—such as the company name, the phone number, and the address—will be the same.

To save the time and effort spent in entering information for these contacts, you can select a contact from the same company, click New Items, and choose "Contact from Same Company." When you create a contact with this command, the company-related information appears automatically in the Contact window, as shown in Exhibit 4-4. You can then enter other details, such as the name and job title.

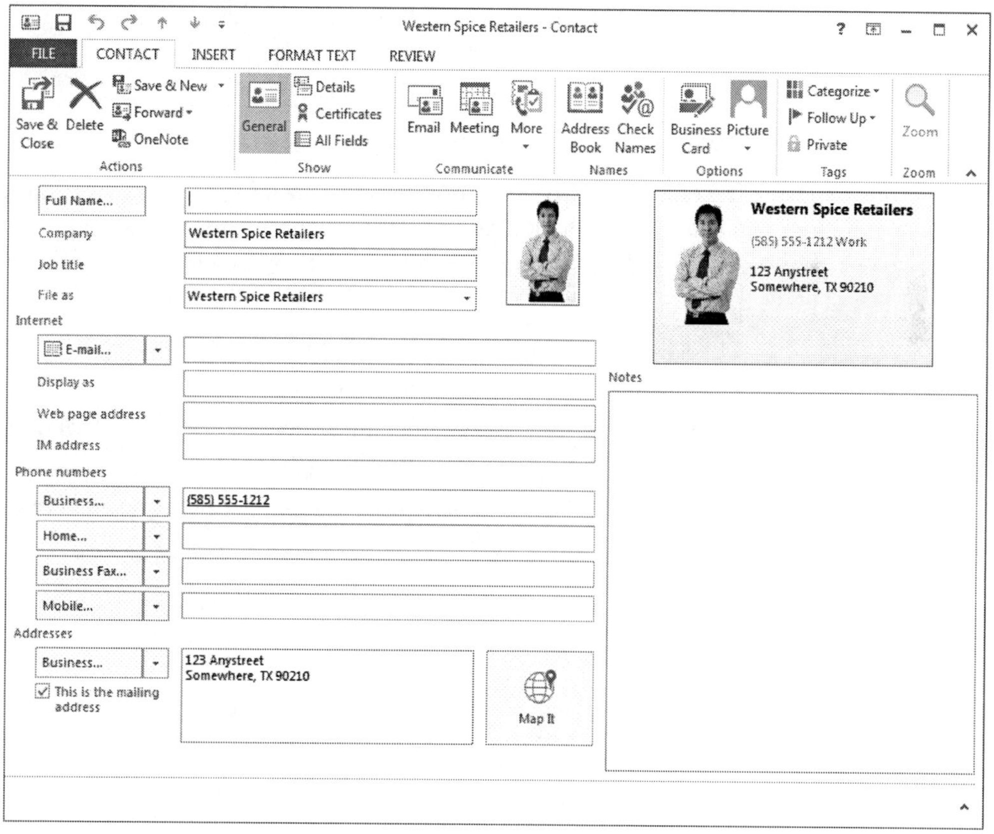

Exhibit 4-4: The new Contact window filled in with company information

Do it! ### A-4: Adding a contact from the same company

Here's how	Here's why
1 Verify that Richard Case is selected	In the People list.
2 On the Home tab, in the New group, click **New Items** and choose **Contact from the Same Company**	You'll add another contact from Western Spice Retailers. The name of the company, the business address, the business phone number, and the picture automatically appear in the Contact window, as shown in Exhibit 4-4.
3 In the Full Name box, enter **Michael Gos**	
In the Job title box, enter **Assistant Buyer**	
On the Contact tab, click **Picture** from the Options group and choose **Remove Picture**	To remove the picture from this contact.
4 Save and close the contact information	Michael Gos appears as a contact in the People list.

Forwarding and saving contacts

Explanation If a colleague needs the information for one of your contacts, instead of typing a contact's information into a message, simply attach the contact to an email message. Create a message and click Attach Item. From the Look in list, select Contacts. Under Items, select the contact you want to attach, and then click OK.

You can also save a contact attachment as a contact record. To do so:

1 Open the email message.
2 Double-click the contact attachment. The Contact window containing the contact's information will appear.
3 Click Save & Close to save the contact in your Contacts.

Do it!

A-5: Forwarding and saving contacts

The files for this activity are in Student Data folder **Unit 4\Topic A**.

Here's how	Here's why
1 Create another contact, from Western Spice Retailers, named **Jill Smith##**	(Click New Items and choose Contact from the Same Company on the Home tab.) Enter your student number for ##.
Set the picture to one of the sample female photos	Click Picture and choose Change Picture. Navigate to the current topic's data folder. Select a photo and click OK.
2 Save and close the contact	
3 Click **Mail**	(From the Navigation bar.) You'll send the Jill Smith contact to your partner.
4 Create a message, addressed to your partner, with the subject **Jill Smith**	
5 Click **Attach Item**	(In the Include group.) You'll attach the Jill Smith contact to the message.
Choose **Business Card, Other Business Cards...**	In Outlook terminology, a contact you send is called a business card.
Select **Smith##, Jill**	
Click **OK**	
6 Send the message	
7 Select the **Jill Smith** message	This is the message from your partner. You can see the contact card in the preview window
8 Double-click where indicated	To Student01 Message Jill Smith02.vcf (5 KB)
	The Contact window appears.
Click **Save & Close**	To save the contact and close the window.
9 Close the message window	If you opened the message rather than previewing it.
10 Click **Contacts**	(From the Navigation bar.) Your partner's Jill Smith## contact is listed with the rest of your contacts.

Using Contacts folder views

Explanation

Outlook offers several views for each folder, such as Inbox or Contacts. A *view* is the way the data appears. In Contacts, the default view is People. In this view, you can see the person's name, company information, phone numbers, fax number, email address, and company address for each contact. From the People card, you can also send an email, get social media updates, or schedule a meeting with the contact.

To change the view for the Contacts folder, select the view you want to use from the Current View list in the ribbon.

Do it!

A-6: Viewing your contacts

Here's how	Here's why
1 Click **Richard Case** from the Contacts list	If necessary.
2 Observe the People pane	Notice there are links where you can schedule a meeting with or send an email to this contact.
3 On the Home tab, in the Current View group, click **Business Card**	Each contact appears as a business address card. These cards are sorted alphabetically and show a few important details, such as a contact's address and phone numbers.
4 To the right of Business Card, click ⬇	To display more view options.
5 Click **Card**	

Case, Richard

Full Name:	Richard Case
Job Title:	Senior Buyer
Company:	Western Spice Retailers
Department:	Marketing
Business:	123 Anystreet Somewhere, TX 90210
Business:	(585) 555-1212
E-mail:	fake@example.com

	(From the Current View group.) To display a list of contact information, without a photo of the contact.
6 Click **Phone**	To display an alphabetized list of all your contacts.
7 Select **List**	To display a list categorized by company and then sorted alphabetically.
8 Select the **Business Card** view	Click the up arrow and then click Business Card.

Customizing electronic business cards

Explanation

You can control what information an electronic business card contains. To do so, double-click the Business Card to open it and click Business Card in the Options group on the Contact tab. This opens the Edit Business Card dialog box, shown in Exhibit 4-5. Here, you can change which content will be displayed by changing the fields that appear on the business card. These fields correspond to the fields in the Contact window.

You can change which fields are displayed on your card by adding or removing them in the Fields list:

- To add a field to the list and display its content on the card, click Add and select a field from the list.

- To prevent a field from being included on the card, select its field name under Fields and click Remove. If you want to add a field back, all you need to do is click Add and select it from the list.

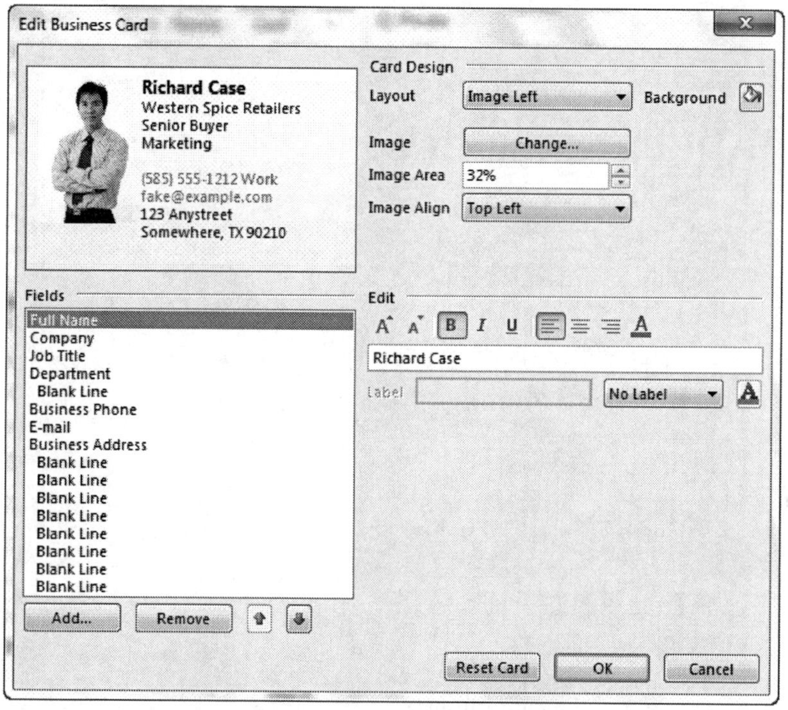

Exhibit 4-5: The Edit Business Card dialog box

Moving fields

With an electronic business card, you're not stuck with any particular order of content display. You can move the fields around. To move a field up or down on the electronic business card, select the field in the list and then click the arrow buttons at the bottom of the dialog box.

Editing field values

You can edit the values of fields in the Edit Business Card dialog box. To do so, select a field and edit the value under Edit. Keep in mind that when you edit the value of a field for the business card, you are also editing it for the associated contact.

If you delete a field value, it will be removed from the electronic business card and from the contact. If you don't want a field displayed on the card, use the Remove button instead.

Do it!

A-7:   Editing an electronic business card

Here's how	Here's why
1 Open the **Richard Case** contact	Double-click the Richard Case business card.
2 On the Contact tab, in the Options group, click **Business Card**	To edit the contact's business card.
3 In the list of fields, select **Department** Click **Remove**	You'll remove the Department field from the business card.
4 In the list of fields, after Business Address, select **Blank Line** Click ⬆	You're selecting the first "Blank Line" item following Business Address.

Fields
Full Name
Company
Job Title
  Blank Line
Business Phone
E-mail
Blank Line
Business Address

To add a blank line before the business address.

5 In the list of fields, select **Business Phone**	You'll edit the label that identifies this field.
6 In the Label box, enter **(W)** Under Edit, click **B**	To make the phone number and its label bold.
From the Label position list, select **Left**	
7 Observe the card preview	

Richard Case
Western Spice Retailers
Senior Buyer

(W) (585) 555-1212
fake@example.com

123 Anystreet
Somewhere, TX 90210

8 Click **OK**	To save your changes and return to the Contact editing window.
9 Click **Save & Close**	This contact's card reflects your changes. The other cards use the default layout.
10 Return to the People view	Click People from the Current View group on the Home tab.

Printing contacts

You can print contacts by using the settings accessible from the File tab, or you can select a single contact, right-click it, and choose Quick Print. If you use the File tab, you can choose from the following styles:

- **Card Style** — The contacts appear as business cards.
- **Small Booklet Style** — The information for multiple contacts is printed, using a small font.
- **Medium Booklet Style** — The information for multiple contacts is printed, using a larger font than the one used with the Small Booklet Style.
- **Memo Style** — Each full contact is printed on a separate page.
- **Phone Directory Style** — Contacts are printed alphabetically by name, with only phone numbers included.

A-8: Printing contacts

Here's how	Here's why
1 Right-click a contact and choose **Quick Print**	To print a single contact in Memo Style.
2 Click the **File** tab and then click **Print**	To display the Print page.
3 Observe the different styles	You have several options for printing single contacts or multiple contacts.
4 Select **Small Booklet Style**	
Click **Print**	To print your contacts.
5 Return to the Home tab	Click the left arrow in the upper-left corner.

Topic B: Address books

This topic covers the following Microsoft Office Specialist exam objectives for Outlook 2013.

#	Objective
4.1	**Create and Manage Contacts**
4.1.3	Import contacts from external sources
4.1.8	Manage multiple address books

Explanation

An *address book* is a collection of names and email addresses. You can use an address book to look up and select names, email addresses, and distribution lists when you address messages.

Built-in address books

There are various address books in Outlook 2013. They include the Global Address List, Contacts (Outlook Address Book), and Contacts (Mobile).

The Global Address List

If you are using an Exchange Server email account, you will have a Global Address List. The *Global Address List* is an address book that contains all of the users, groups, and distribution-list email addresses in your organization. All users in an organization have access to the Global Address List. It is created and maintained by your email administrator. You cannot edit this address book.

Contacts

Each user has a private address book called Contacts. The Contacts list is created automatically, though by default it is empty. You can use Contacts to keep email addresses and other contact details for the people with whom you frequently communicate, who are not in your Global Address List.

Accessing address books

You can access address books by using various techniques. These include the following:

- Create an email message. On the Ribbon, click Address Book to open the Select Names dialog box, shown in Exhibit 4-6. From the Address Book list, select the address book you want to view.

- Create an email message. Click the To button. From the Address Book list, select the address book you want to view.

Select Names: Global Address List

Search: ⦿ Name only ○ More columns   **Address Book**

[   ] [Go]   Global Address List - Student01@outlande ▾   Advanced Find

Name	Title	Business Phone	Location
Administrator			
Conference Room A			
Instructor			
Student01			
Student02			
Student03			
Student04			

[To ->] [   ]
[Cc ->] [   ]
[Bcc ->] [   ]

[OK] [Cancel]

Exhibit 4-6: The Select Names dialog box

Auto-complete list

In addition to selecting a name or email address from an address book, Outlook maintains an auto-complete list. As you type into the To, Cc, or Bcc box, Outlook checks the auto-complete list for a match. If a match is found as you type, the Display Name and email address is filled in.

If a name appears in the auto-complete list that you no longer want, you can delete it by clicking the delete (x) button next to the name in the list. If you no longer wish to have Outlook suggest recipients, you can turn off the auto-complete list by selecting Options from the File tab and clearing the Use Auto-Complete List to suggest names when typing in the To, Cc, and Bcc option from the Send messages section.

B-1: Viewing address books

Here's how	Here's why
1 Create a message	
2 In the Names group on the Ribbon, click **Address Book**	This is one method for opening the address book.
Click **Cancel**	
3 Click **To**	This is another way to open the address book.
Click **Cancel**	
4 In the To box, enter **bit-bucket@test.smtp.org**	This is a special email address created for testing. Mail sent to it is simply discarded.
5 Enter a subject and message of your choice	This is a test message and won't be read by anyone.
Click **Send**	
6 Create a message	
7 In the To box, enter **bit**	As soon as you begin typing an address, Outlook checks the auto-complete list for a potential match. Outlook suggests the bit-bucket@test.smtp.org address.
Click ⊠	
	Next to the bit-bucket@test.smtp.org email address. This address is removed from the auto-complete list.
Close the Message window without sending or saving the message	
8 On the Home tab, click **New Items** and choose **Email Message**	In the New group.
9 In the To box, enter **bit**	Because you deleted it from the auto-complete list, Outlook no longer suggests the bit-bucket@test.smtp.org address.
Press (ESC)	
Click **No**	To close the Message window without sending or saving the message.

Importing contacts

Explanation

You can import contacts from Excel spreadsheets, ACT! Contact Manager files, comma-separated value (.csv) files, VCard (.vcf) files, and files exported from Outlook Express or Eudora. For example, you might import contacts if you're switching from another email program to Outlook.

The exact steps vary by the type of file you're importing. But in general, follow these steps to import contact data:

1 Click the File tab and then click Open & Export.

2 Click Import/Export to open the Import and Export Wizard.

3 Select the action you want to perform. For example, to import an Excel spreadsheet, select "Import from another program or file." Click Next.

4 Follow the remaining steps in the Import and Export Wizard to import the data. Typically, you will need to specify the type of data you're importing and where you want the imported data to reside within Outlook.

When importing data from file formats other than specific Outlook address book formats (Excel spreadsheets, for example), you might need to manage the fields into which your data is imported. Outlook takes its "best guess" by examining the field names associated with each column. By using the Map Custom Fields dialog box, shown in Exhibit 4-7, you can carefully control the import.

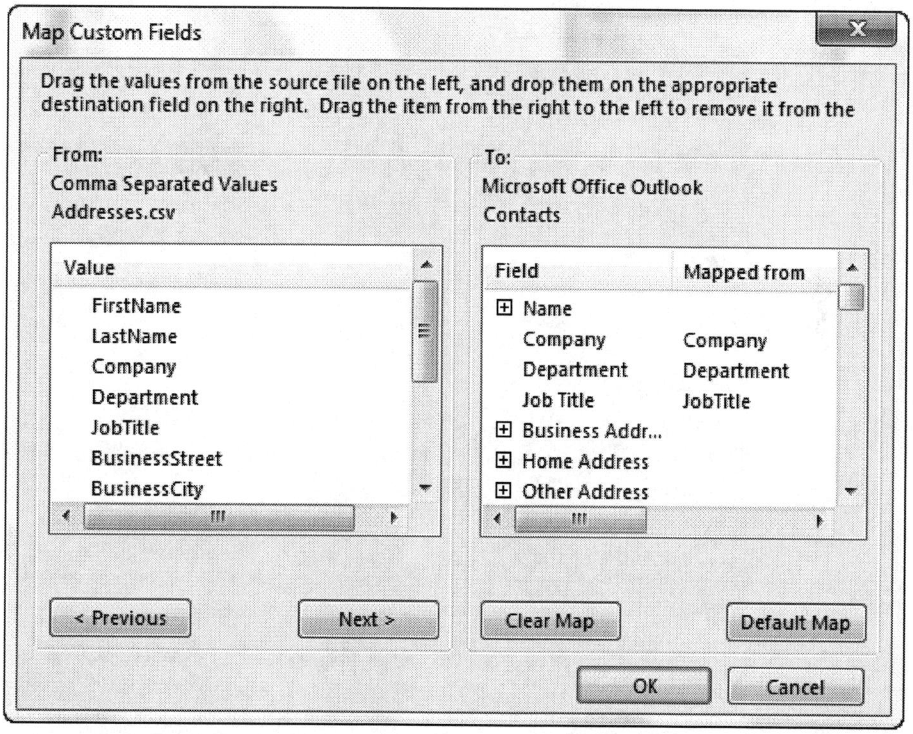

Exhibit 4-7: You use this dialog box to map the fields in a spreadsheet to the fields in your Outlook Contacts

Do it!

B-2:   Importing contact data from Excel

The files for this activity are in Student Data folder **Unit 4\Topic B**.

Here's how	Here's why
1 Click the **File** tab and click **Open & Export**	
2 Click **Import/Export**	To open the Import and Export Wizard.
3 Select **Import from another program or file**	If necessary. You'll import a CSV file that was exported from an Excel spreadsheet.
Click **Next**	
4 Select **Comma Separated Values**	To specify what type of file you're importing your data from.
Click **Next**	
5 Click **Browse**	
Navigate to the current topic folder and select **Addresses.csv**	To specify which file to import.
Click **OK**	
6 Observe the import options	Options ○ Replace duplicates with items imported ● Allow duplicates to be created ○ Do not import duplicate items
Click **Next**	
7 In the "Select the destination folder" list, scroll up	The Contacts folder should be selected.
Click **Next**	The import summary is displayed.
8 Click **Map Custom Fields**	Using the Map Custom Fields dialog box, you can control which columns of Excel data are imported to which Outlook contact fields.
Click **Cancel**	To leave the field mapping settings at their default values.
9 Click **Finish**	To import the data. The contacts are imported to your Contacts folder.

Topic C: Using contact groups

This topic covers the following Microsoft Office Specialist exam objectives for Outlook 2013.

#	Objective
4.2	**Create and Manage Groups**
4.2.1	Create new contact groups
4.2.2	Add contacts to existing groups
4.2.3	Add notes to a group
4.2.4	Update contacts within groups
4.2.5	Delete groups
4.2.6	Delete group members

Explanation

Contact groups simplify the steps you must take to email a group of people. Normally, you would need to add each recipient to the To box of your message. Instead, you can address the message to your contact group, and Outlook will send copies to every member of the group.

A *contact group*, formerly known as a distribution list, is a collection of email addresses. You assign a name to a contact group. To send email to members of the group, address your message to the group's name.

Creating contact groups

Your Exchange administrator can create contact groups in the Global Address List. You can create them in your personal Contacts folder.

To create a contact group in your Contacts folder:

1 On the Home tab, in the New group, click New Contact Group to open a new Contact Group window, as shown in Exhibit 4-8.

2 In the Name box, enter the name you want to use for the group.

3 In the Members group on the Contact Group tab, click Add Members. Then choose one of these three options:

   • **From Outlook Contacts** — Displays names from your local Contacts list.

   • **From Address Book** — Displays names from the global Exchange address book.

   • **New E-mail Contact** — Enables you to enter an email address directly.

4 Select a member from the Name list and click Members.

5 Repeat step 4 until all the desired members are selected. Then click OK.

6 In the Actions group, click Save & Close.

If you have multiple members to add, you can select them in step 4 by pressing Ctrl, clicking each member you want to include, and clicking Members. You also can enter email addresses by typing them in the Members box at the bottom of the dialog box. Enter a semicolon (;) after each member you add manually.

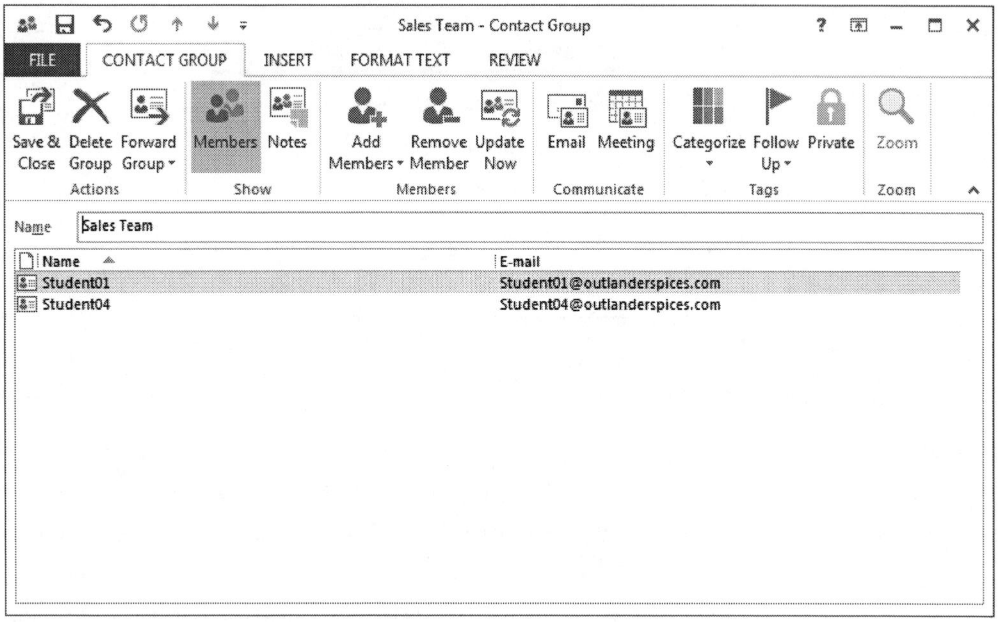

Exhibit 4-8: The Sales Team - Contact Group window

Using contact groups

One way to send a message to a contact group is to right-click the group from the Business Card view and choose Create, Email. This opens a new Message window. In the To box, the name of the contact group is underlined, indicating that the group is valid. You can then compose and send the message, which will be delivered to everyone in the group.

Another way to send a message to a contact group is to create an email message and enter the name of the contact group in the To box. As you type the first few letters of the group's name, the rest of the name will appear, and you can press Enter to enter it.

Do it!   ## C-1:   Creating and using a contact group

Here's how	Here's why
1 Click **Contacts**	(If necessary.) From the Navigation bar.
2 On the Home tab, click **New Contact Group**	In the New group.
3 In the Name box, enter **Sales Team**	This will be the name of your contact group.
4 In the Members group, click **Add Members** and choose **From Address Book**	To open the Select Members dialog box. You'll add members to the Sales Team group.
From the Name list, select **Student01**	
Click **Members**	To add Student01 to your contact group.
5 Add Student04	Select Student04 and click Members.
Click **OK**	To close the Select Members dialog box. The Contact Group window appears, as shown in Exhibit 4-8.
6 Click **Save & Close**	To save the Sales Team contact group. It now appears as a contact in the Contacts list.
7 Create a new message	Choose E-mail Message from the New Items list in the New group on the Home tab.
From the To box, type **sa** and select **Sales Team**	Sales Team appears in the To box. The name has been automatically checked and validated against the Global Address List.
8 Send the message with the subject **Distribution Sales Report**	

Modifying contact groups

Explanation
After you've created a contact group, you might need to add or remove members. You also might need to change a member's information, such as by adding a new email address or phone number.

To add a new member to the contact group:

1 Open the contact group.
2 On the Contact Group tab, in the Members group, click Add Members and choose the appropriate source.
3 Select or add the contact.
4 Click Save & Close.

If you want to add a member who is already in your address book, then open the contact group, click Add Members, and choose From Address Book. Select the member you want to add, click Members, and click OK.

To remove a member from the contact group, open the group. Select the member you want to remove and click Remove Member in the Members group.

Updating contact details

Contact details change. If you update an entry in your contacts, that information will not be automatically reflected in your contact group. You should make sure to update your contact group after modifying contact details. To do so:

1 Open the contact group.
2 On the Contact Group tab, in the Members group, click Update Now.

When editing your contact group, you can update a member's details with a simple double-click as long as he or she is not in your organization. Otherwise, you must add her or him to your contacts list first and then update the information.

To update a member's information:

1 Open the contact group.
2 Double-click the member's name.

   If he or she is not in your organization, this will open the Contact window, where you can edit this person's details.

3 Enter the new information. Click Save & Close to return to the Contact Group window.
4 Click Save & Close.

To send the updated information to the entire contact group:

1 Create an email message, click To, locate and double-click the contact group, and click OK.
2 In the Include group, click Attach Item.
3 From the Look in list, select Contacts.
4 From the Items list, select the contact group. Click OK.
5 Complete and send the message.

Do it!

C-2:   Modifying a contact group

Here's how	Here's why
1 Activate Contacts	(If necessary.) You'll add and remove members of the Sales Team contact group.
2 Double-click the **Sales Team** contact group	To open the Sales Team Contact Group window.
3 Click **Add Members** and choose **From Outlook Contacts**	
Select **Richard Case**	
Click **Members** and click **OK**	
4 Double-click **Richard Case**	In the list of members. He is not in your organization, so the Contact window opens.
Edit the email address to be **rcase@westernspices.com**	
Click **Save & Close**	To save the new information.
5 Select **Student04**	You'll remove this member from the contact group.
Click **Remove Member**	In the Members group on the Ribbon.
6 Click **Save & Close**	Student01 is listed with your other contacts.

Forwarding a contact group

Explanation

Once you create a contact group, you can share it with other users. To share a contact group you've created:

1   Click Contacts.
2   Select the group you want to share.
3   On the Home tab, in the Share group, click Forward Contact and choose "As an Outlook Contact."
4   In the To: field, enter the email addresses of the person or persons you want to share the contact group with.
5   Click Send.

If you receive a shared contact group in email, you can add it to your Contacts by dragging the attachment from the message to your Contacts in the Folder pane.

C-3: Forwarding a contact group

Here's how	Here's why
1 Click **Contacts**	If necessary.
2 Click **New Contact Group**	You'll quickly create a contact group to use for the activities in this topic.
3 In the Name box, type your first name, followed by **'s Group**	For example, "Joe's Group."
4 Click **Add Members** and choose **From Address Book**	
5 Add your partner's Student## account and the instructor account Click **OK**	
6 Click **Save and Close**	
7 Select the group you just created	
8 Click **Forward Contact** and choose **As an Outlook Contact**	
9 Send the message to your partner's Student## account	
10 When the message from your partner arrives, select it	
11 Double-click the group email attachment	From the Reading pane.
12 Click the **File** tab	You'll copy the email group to the Contacts folder.
Click the **Move to Folder** button and select **Copy to Folder...** Select the Contacts folder for your mailbox and click OK	
13 Select **Contacts**	Your partner's group has been saved in your Contacts.

Contact group notes

Explanation

You can add descriptive notes to contact groups. To do so:

1   Open the contact group you want to add a note to.

2   In the Show group, click Notes.

3   Enter the descriptive text you want to add regarding the group.

4   Click Save & Close.

To view any notes attached to a contact group, open the contact group and click Notes. Any notes that have been entered are displayed as shown in Exhibit 4-9. The notes can be edited in this window.

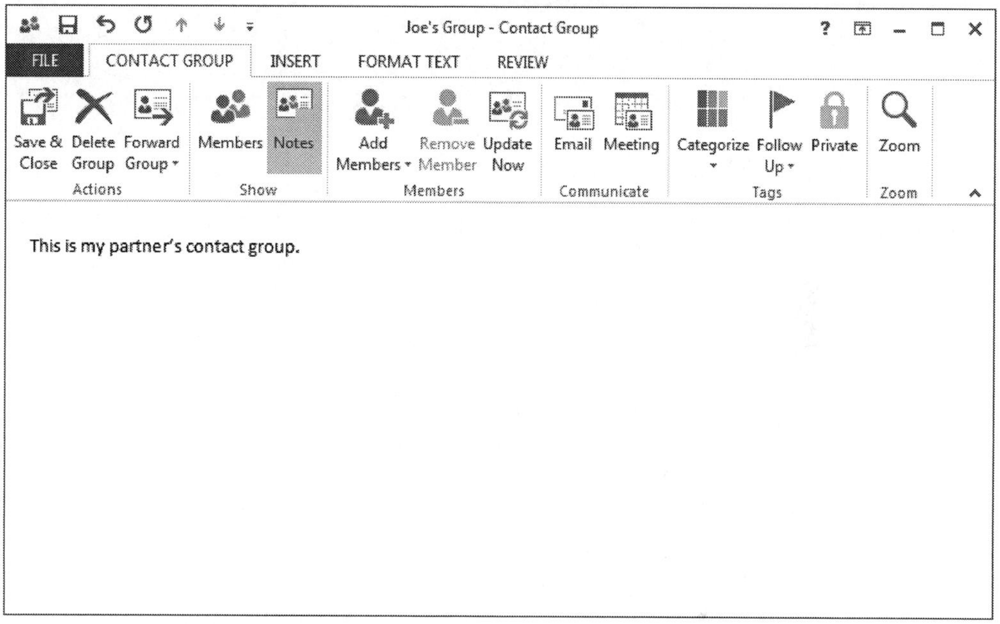

Exhibit 4-9: Notes for a contact group

Do it!

C-4:   Adding contact group notes

Here's how	Here's why
1 In Contacts, double-click the contact group your partner sent you	
2 In the Show group, click **Notes**	
3 Type **This is my partner's contact group.**	
4 Click **Save & Close**	

Deleting a contact group

Explanation When you no longer need a contact group, you can delete it. Select the contact group you want to delete and click Delete.

Do it!

C-5: Deleting a contact group

Here's how	Here's why
1 Select your partner's contact group	
2 Click **Delete**	Notice that you aren't prompted to confirm the deletion. If you inadvertently delete a contact or contact group, use the Undo button to get it back.

Unit summary: Contacts

Topic A   In this topic, you used the Contacts folder to **create** and **edit contacts**. You also added contacts from the same company. Then you used different **views** of your Contacts folder. In addition, you edited and formatted a contact's **electronic business card**. Finally, you **printed** a list of contacts.

Topic B   In this topic, you learned about the **Outlook address books**: Global Address List, and Contacts. You also learned how to **import** contacts from an Excel spreadsheet.

Topic C   In this topic, you created and used **contact groups**, which make it easier to send a message to multiple recipients. You also added and removed members of a contact group and updated member information. You learned how to share a contact group with other Outlook users by forwarding it. You learned how to add descriptive notes to a contact group, and you learned how to **delete** a contact group that you no longer need.

Review questions

1 What steps do you follow to create a contact?

2 How do you edit a contact?

3 Name the five views available in the Contacts folder.

4 How do you create a new contact that works for the same company as one of your previous contacts?

5 What is the advantage of creating a contact group?

6 How do you send a message to a contact group?

7 How do you create an electronic business card?

8 Can you modify the information shown in an electronic business card?

9 How do you send an electronic business card to another person?

10 Which address book is maintained by an organization's email administrator and cannot be edited by users?

   A Global Address List

   B Contacts

   C Personal Address Book

   D Outlook Address Book

11 Which address book is directly created and maintained by the user?

   A Global Address List

   B Public Address Book

   C Contacts

   D Personal Address Book

12 When you are importing data from file formats other than Outlook address book formats (Excel spreadsheets, for example), what feature do you use to manage the fields into which your data is imported?

   A Add/Remove Fields

   B Change Destination

   C Manage Data Fields

   D Map Custom Fields

13 You can share a contact group with another user by _____ it.

14 True or false? You can add descriptive text for a contact group.

Independent practice activity

In this activity, you'll add contacts, create a contact group, and address a new message to a specified contact group.

1 Add Peter Greenfield's contact information as shown in Exhibit 4-10. Save the contact information.

2 Add **Scott Bates** as a new contact from the same company as Peter Greenfield, and specify his job title as **Marketing Director**. Save the contact information.

3 Create a contact group with the name **Purchase Team**. Add Student03 and Student04 as members. Save the information.

4 Send a message to Purchase Team with the subject **Requirements** and a brief message of your choice.

5 Add the email address **pgreenfield@wonderlandhotels.com** to the Peter Greenfield contact.

6 On Peter Greenfield's electronic business card, change the label for the phone number to **Phone:** and move it to the left side.

7 Save and close the business card.

8 Save and close the contact.

9 Import the contacts from IPA Addresses.xls into your Contacts folder.

10 Create a contact group called **Dover Spice Works**.

11 Add all contacts who work for Dover Spice Works to the group. (Their email addresses end in @doverspiceworks.com.)

12 Add the following note to the Dover Spice Works group: **Outlander Spices subsidiary in Cloverdale California**.

13 Forward the Dover Spice Works contact group to your partner.

Exhibit 4-10: The contact information to be added in Step 1

Unit 5
Tasks

Complete this unit, and you'll know how to:

A Use the Tasks list to create, edit, and delete single and recurring tasks; insert a task into a message and view your tasks.

B Use the Tasks list to assign tasks, accept or decline a task request, send a status report, and track the completion of an assigned task.

Topic A: Working with tasks

This topic covers the following Microsoft Office Specialist exam objectives for
Outlook 2013.

#	Objective
3.4	**Create and Manage Notes, Tasks, and Journals**
3.4.1	Create and manage tasks

Explanation

In Outlook, a *task* is an activity that must be completed within a specified period of
time. A task has a current *status*, which can be In Progress, Not Started, Waiting on
someone else, Deferred, or Completed. You can assign a Low, Normal, or High priority
to a task, and you can track its completion by setting a percent-complete value.

Youcan create tasks and monitor their status in the *Task list*. After creating a task, you
can edit or delete it. In addition, you can send a task through email as an attachment.

The Task list stores the tasks you need to perform—both those you created and those
that another person has assigned to you. To display the Tasks folder, click Tasks in the
Folder pane.

Exhibit 5-1 shows the Outlook window with Tasks active. The list of tasks appears in
the Tasks list. When you click on a task, the task's details appear in the Reading pane.

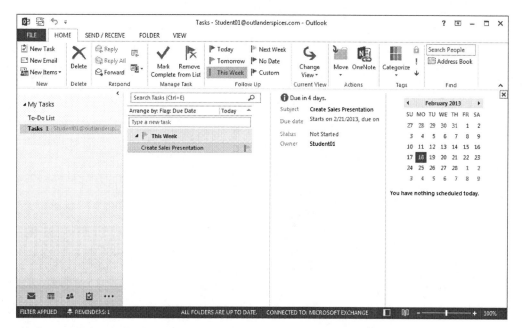

Exhibit 5-1: The Tasks list and Reading pane

Do it!   **A-1: Exploring the To-Do bar and Tasks view**

Here's how	Here's why
1 From the Navigation bar, click [icon]	To show the Calendar view.
2 Click the **View** tab	You'll view and customize the To-Do bar for the Calendar view. .
From the Layout group, click **To-Do Bar**	
Select **Tasks**	From the To-Do bar list. The Tasks list is shown to the right of the Calendar on the To-Do bar.
3 From the Navigation bar, click [icon]	
4 Observe the Tasks list	Search Tasks (Ctrl+E) 🔎 Arrange by: Flag: Due Date | Today ▲ Type a new task We didn't find anything to show here. You have no tasks defined. Using the boxes in the Tasks list, you can search for, change your view of, and create tasks.
5 Click the **View** tab	
6 In the Current View group, click **Change View**	Detailed Simple List To-Do List Prioritized Active Completed Today Next 7 Days Overdue Assigned Server Tasks Manage Views... Save Current View As a New View... Apply Current View to Other Task Folders... To display a list of view options. To-Do List is the default view.
Press (ESC)	

Creating and deleting tasks

Explanation

There are several ways you can create a task:

- With Tasks active, click New Task on the Home tab. With this method, you will open a Task window, as shown in Exhibit 5-2.
- With Tasks active, enter a task title in the "Type a new task" box in the Task list or To-Do bar (if displayed). The Task window is not displayed; double-click your task to open it.
- Flag an email message to add it to your To-Do Bar's Task list. The Task window is not displayed; double-click your task to open it.

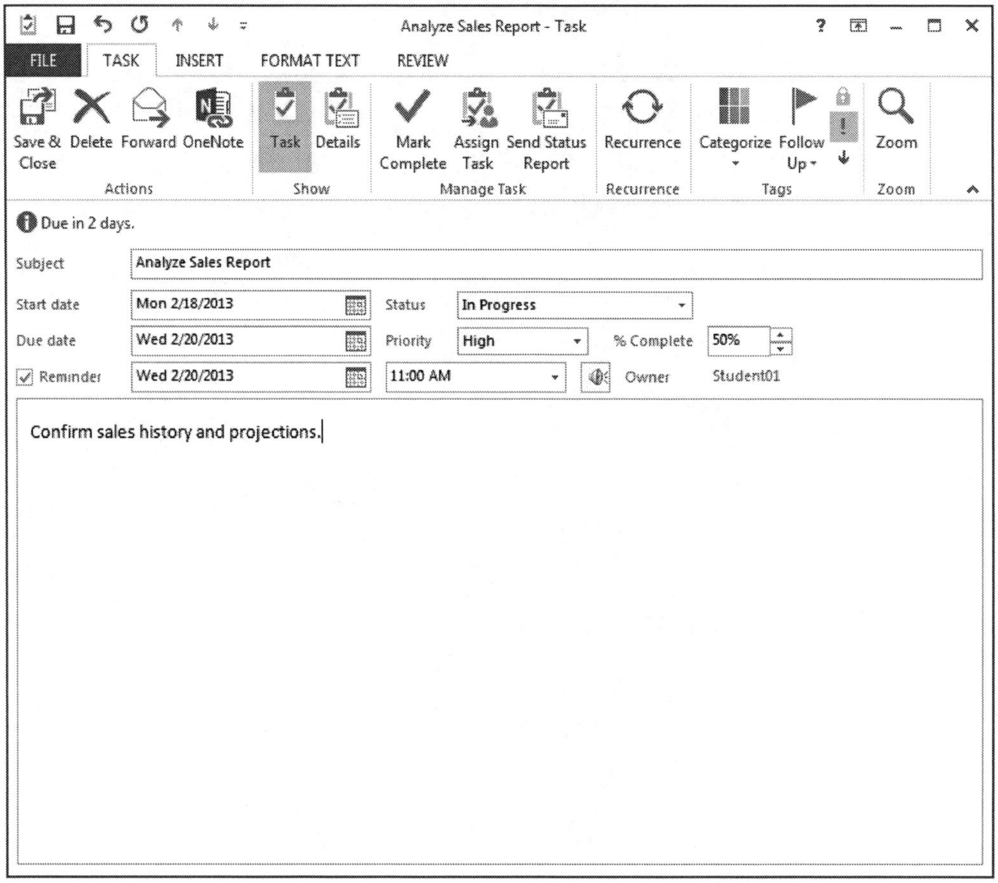

Exhibit 5-2: A new Task window

When creating or editing a task, you can enter details, such as a Start date, Due date, Status, Priority, % Complete, and Reminder. (See Exhibit 5-2 for examples.) After entering your task details, click Save & Close.

You can quickly create tasks by using the "Type a new task" box in the Tasks list or the To-Do bar (if displayed). When you do so, the task will not be assigned a date for the due date and start date. The priority will be set to Normal, and the status will be set to Not Started. Double-click the task to edit it.

The Task window

In the new Task window, the Show group on the Task tab contains two buttons: Task and Details. Click the Task button if you want to enter such information as the subject, start and end dates, status, and priority. Click the Details button if you want to enter such information as the total work estimated, the actual time taken, and expenses incurred to complete the task.

Deleting a task

Deleting a task removes it from your Tasks list. Deleting a task is different from marking it as completed. When you mark a task as completed, Outlook retains a record of the work you've done. When you delete a task, it is moved to your Deleted Items folder.

To delete a task, do any of the following:

- Select the task and then click Delete on the Home tab.
- Right-click the task and choose Delete.
- Double-click the task to open the Task window. Click Delete on the Task tab.

Do it!

A-2:   Creating and deleting tasks

Here's how	Here's why
1 On the Home tab, click **New Task**	To open a new Task window. You'll create a task for analyzing a sales report. The report has to be analyzed and the feedback has to be sent within two days.
2 In the Subject box, enter **Analyze Sales Report**	To specify the subject of the task.
3 Observe the Start and Due dates	They are blank by default.
4 Click the arrow next to the Start date box	To display the Date Navigator.
Select today's date	You'll start this task today.
5 Set the Due date to two days after the current date	ⓘ Due in 2 days. Subject Analyze Sales Report
	To specify the due date. The InfoBar indicates that the task is due in two days.
6 From the Status list, select **In Progress**	To specify that this task is in progress.
7 From the Priority list, select **High**	To specify the importance of the task.

8	Edit the % Complete box to read **50%**	To specify the percentage of the task that is completed.
9	Check **Reminder**	To set a reminder for the task. By default, you will be reminded on the due date. You could set another date.
10	From the Reminder time list, select **11:00 AM**	To specify the time when the reminder should appear.
11	In the description box, enter **Confirm sales history and projections.**	To enter a description of what this task entails.
12	Click **Save & Close**	The task appears in the Task list, and a preview of it appears in the Reading pane.
13	In the Task list, in the "Type a new task" box, type **Create Sales Presentation**	
	Press ⏎ ENTER	

◢ ⯈ No Date	
Create Sales Presentation	☐ ⯈

		Your task is created, with No Date set as its due date.
14	Create a task named **Lunch with Bob**	Enter it in the "Type a new task" box.
15	In the Task list, select **Lunch with Bob**	You'll delete this task because it would be more appropriate to create this type of item as a Calendar entry rather than as a task.
	Click **Delete**	(On the Home tab.) To delete the task.

Editing tasks

Explanation

As you work on your tasks, the status or the percentage completed will change. To reflect these changes, you'll need to edit the task information. You can edit such information as the status, the due date, and the percentage of completion. You can also mark tasks as private.

To edit a task:

1 Open the task.
2 Change the due date, status, priority, and percent complete, as needed.
3 Click Save & Close.

Do it!

A-3:   Editing a task

Here's how	Here's why
1 In the Tasks list, double-click **Create Sales Presentation**	You'll edit this task.
2 Set the start date to be three days from now	
3 Set the due date to be four days from now	
4 From the Status list, select **Deferred**	To specify that the task has been delayed or postponed.
5 Save and close the task	The task changes are reflected in the Folder Contents list.

Setting up recurring tasks

Explanation

A *recurring task* is a task that needs to be performed on a regular basis. To create a recurring task, you need to specify the pattern in which the task recurs. For example, you can create a task for the first Monday of every month or the fourth Wednesday of every April. This is called the *recurrence pattern*, which can be annual, monthly, weekly, or daily. You also need to specify the *range of recurrence*, which indicates the starting and ending dates for the recurring task, as shown in Exhibit 5-3.

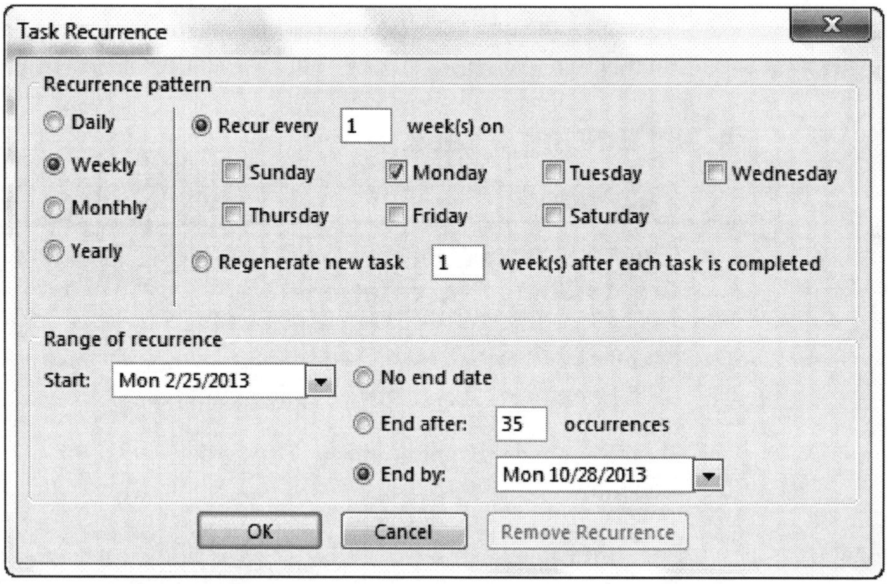

Exhibit 5-3: Scheduling a recurring task

To create a recurring task:

1 Open a new Task window.

2 Enter the necessary information.

3 On the Task tab, in the Recurrence group, click Recurrence to open the Task Recurrence dialog box.

4 Specify settings for the recurrence pattern and click OK.

5 Click Save & Close.

Do it!   **A-4:   Adding a recurring task**

Here's how	Here's why
1 Create a task with the subject **Generate Sales Report**	Open a new Task window, and enter the subject "Generate Sales Report."
	You need to send a sales report to a manager every Monday for the next six months. Instead of creating a task every week, you'll create a recurring task.
Specify the start date as next Monday	Click the arrow next to the Start date box to display the Date Navigator, and select the next Monday.
2 On the Task tab, click **Recurrence**	(In the Recurrence group.) To open the Task Recurrence dialog box.
3 Under Recurrence pattern, select **Weekly**	(If necessary.) To specify that this task has to be performed every week.
Select **Recur every**	If necessary.
Enter **1**	If necessary.
Check **Monday**	If necessary.
4 Examine the options under "Range of recurrence"	You can specify the start and end dates of the recurrence period. You specify the start date in the Start box. By default, no end date is selected. If you know the number of occurrences, use the "End after" option to specify that number. If the recurring task ends on a specific date, use the "End by" option.
Select **End by**	
Display the Date Navigator and select the Monday six months from the start date	Click the arrow next to the End by box to display the Date Navigator.
5 Click **OK**	

> **ⓘ** Due in 7 days.
> Starts every Monday effective 2/25/2013 until 10/28/2013.
>
> Subject   Generate Sales Report

	To close the Task Recurrence dialog box and save the settings. The InfoBar summarizes the details of the recurring task.
6 Save the task	The task is added to the Next Week section in the Task list.

Switching task views

Explanation

Views are used to arrange and manage tasks. Outlook provides several views for tasks, such as Active Tasks and Overdue Tasks. Each view displays tasks in a specific way. For example, Active Tasks view shows you all of the current tasks. You can also view tasks by the person responsible and by completion date.

To switch to a different view, you select it from the Change View list in the Current View group on the Home tab, as shown in Exhibit 5-4.

Exhibit 5-4: Task views

Do it!

A-5: Viewing tasks

Here's how	Here's why
1 Click **Tasks**	(If necessary.) From the Folder pane.
2 In the Current View group, click **Change View**	(If necessary.) To display the view options.
3 Click **Detailed**	This view includes the status, due date, and more information.
4 Explore each of the other views	Click Change View and select each of the other views.
5 Switch to Simple List view	
6 Click **To-Do List**	From the Folder pane.

Marking tasks as completed

Explanation

When you complete a task, you change its status to Complete. Outlook then marks the task as completed. There are several ways to mark a task as completed:

- In the Task list, select the task and click Mark Complete on the Home tab.
- In the Task list or the To-Do Bar's Task list, right-click the task and choose Mark Complete from the shortcut menu.
- Open the task and enter "100%" in the % Complete box.
- Open the task and select Completed from the Status list.
- In the Detailed or Simple List Tasks view, check the checkbox next to the task name.

Completed tasks are not shown in the To-Do list or the To-Do Bar. In the Detailed or Simple List Tasks view, completed tasks are formatted with a strikethrough line across their names.

Do it!

A-6: Marking a task as completed

Here's how	Here's why
1 Select the **Analyze Sales Report** task	
2 Click **Mark Complete**	(On the Home tab.) The task is removed from the Tasks list.
3 In the Folder pane, beneath My Tasks, click **Tasks**	▲ My Tasks To-Do List **Tasks** Stud To change to Tasks view. The completed task is shown in this view.
4 Double-click the **Analyze Sales Report** task	To open it for editing.
5 Edit the % Complete box to read **25%**	
Press TAB	The Status box now displays In Progress.
6 Save the task	It is no longer formatted with strikethrough text; it is not marked as completed.
7 Check the box next to the Analyze Sales Report task	To mark it as completed.
8 View the completed task	☑ ~~Analyze Sales Report~~ ☑ ☐ Create Sales Presentation The checkmark and strikethrough indicate that the task has been completed.

Topic B: Managing tasks

This topic covers the following Microsoft Office Specialist exam objectives for Outlook 2013.

#	Objective
1.3	**Print and Save Information in Outlook**
1.3.6	Print tasks
3.4	**Create and Manage Notes, Tasks, and Journals**
3.4.5	Update task status

Explanation

If you're working on a team project, you might need to assign a task to someone else on the team. It might be a task that you cannot finish or one that is more suited to another person. You can create the task and then assign it to someone else by sending a *task request* in an email message. The recipient can accept or decline a task request. If the recipient accepts the task, it's added to the recipient's task list, and the recipient becomes the new owner of the task.

Assigning tasks

When you assign a task, you might want to track its status. You can do this by keeping an updated copy of the task in your task list and by asking for a status report when the task is completed.

You can also keep a project team updated on your tasks. While you are working on a task, you can send status reports to team members.

To assign a task:

1 Open a task or create a new one.

2 In the Manage Task group on the Task tab, click the Assign Task button.

3 In the To box, enter the email address of the person to whom you want to assign the task.

4 If you want to keep a copy of the task, check "Keep an updated copy of this task on my task list."

5 To be notified when the recipient marks the task as completed, check "Send me a status report when this task is complete."

6 Click Send.

Do it!   **B-1:   Assigning a task**

Here's how	Here's why
1 Create a task with the subject **xx: Update Sales Web site**	Where *xx* is your partner's lab station number. You'll assign the task of updating the Sales Web site to your partner.
2 From the Start date list, select the first Tuesday of the next month From the Due date list, select the last Tuesday of the next month	
3 Click **Details**	(In the Show group on the Task tab.) To display the Details options.
Edit the Total work box to read **200 hours**	To specify the total time needed for the task.
4 Click **Assign Task**	(In the Manage Task group on the Task tab.) You'll send this task to your partner.
Address the message to your partner	
5 Verify that **Keep an updated copy of this task on my task list** is checked	When the assignee accepts the task, the task will be moved to that person's Tasks list and you'll retain a copy of it.
6 Verify that **Send me a status report when this task is complete** is checked	To specify that you want to receive a message when the task is completed.
7 Click **Send**	To send the task request message to your partner. The task is shown with the others in your task list.
8 Check your messages	(View your Inbox.) The task assignment should be listed in your Inbox.

Accepting or declining assigned tasks

Explanation If you send a task request to someone and he or she accepts it, the task is no longer yours. The recipient becomes the temporary owner of the task. When the recipient accepts the task, a message appears in your Inbox, stating that the task request has been accepted and ownership passes to the person who accepted the task.

To accept a task request:

1 Open or preview the task request email message.
2 Click Accept.
3 Send a message that informs the sender that you are accepting the task.

When you accept a task, it will appear in your Task list.

To decline a task request:

1 Open or preview the task request email message.
2 Click Decline.
3 Send a message that informs the sender that you are declining the task.

If you are the creator of a task that is declined, you'll receive a message stating that the task request has been declined. To become the owner of the declined task, open it and click Return to Task List in the Manage Task group on the Ribbon.

Delegating assigned tasks

There might be occasions when you are assigned a task that someone else is better suited to handle. In that case, you can *delegate,* or send, the task to someone else. When the recipient accepts the task, he or she owns it.

To delegate a task:

1 Open the task request that you want to delegate.
2 In the Manage Task group on the Task tab, click Assign Task.
3 In the To box, enter the new recipient's name.
4 Check or clear the desired options to keep a copy of the task in your Tasks folder and/or to receive a status report when the task is complete.
5 Click Send.

Task folders

When you have multiple tasks, it can be easier to keep track of them by grouping related tasks into a single folder. For example, if you have several tasks related to a business trip, you can create a folder and move or copy the tasks to that folder so all tasks for the trip are together and easy to track.

To create a folder to organize tasks:

1 In the Folder pane, right-click Tasks and choose New Folder.
2 Name the folder and click OK.
3 In the Task list, select the tasks you want to move to the folder, and drag them to the folder in the Folder pane.

Do it!   **B-2: Accepting and declining a task request**

Here's how	Here's why
1 Switch to the Mail view	(If necessary.) From the Navigation bar, click the Mail button.
2 Select the **Task Request: *yy*: Update Sales Web site** message	Where *yy* is your student number.
3 Observe the Accept and Decline buttons	✓ Accept ✗ Decline These buttons are shown at the top of the message preview in the Reading pane.
4 Double-click the **Task Request: *yy*: Update Sales Web site** message	To open it.
Observe the Accept and Decline buttons	The Accept and Decline buttons are in the Respond group on the Ribbon.
5 Click **Accept**	To accept the task.
Verify that **Send the response now** is selected	
Click **OK**	To accept the task and notify the sender that you are accepting it.
6 From the Navigation bar, click **Tasks**	To verify that the task now appears in your Tasks folder. The task you created and assigned to your partner is also listed—that task has your partner's number in the subject.
7 In the Folder pane, right-click **Tasks** and choose **New Folder...**	
Name the folder **Web Site Work** and click **OK**	The new folder is created below the Tasks folder.
8 Right-click the **Update Sales Web site** task that was sent to you, and hold down the right mouse button	
Drag the task to the Web Site Work folder and choose **Move**	To move the task to the new folder. You can now keep tasks related to the Web site together in one location.

9	Click **Change View** and choose **Assigned**	(From the Current View group.) To view tasks in your list that are assigned to other people.
	Click **Change View** and choose **Simple List**	
10	Create a task with the subject *xx*: **Sales meeting agenda**	Where *xx* is your partner's number.
	Click **Assign Task**	You'll assign the task to your partner.
	Address and send the task to your partner	
11	View your Inbox	
12	Select the **Task Request:** *yy*: **Sales meeting agenda** message	Or open it.
	Click **Decline**	To decline the task.
	Select **Edit the response before sending**	To be able to enter a message about why you are declining the task.
	Click **OK**	
13	In the message area, enter **I will be on vacation next week.**	
	Click **Send**	
14	Check your Inbox for task response messages	

For step 14:

> ⓘ Declined by STUDENT02 on 2/18/2013 4:06 PM.
>
> Subject   02:Sales meeting agenda
> Due date None
> Status   Not Started   Priority   Normal
> Owner   Student01
>
> I will be on vacation next week.

Status reports

Explanation

Often you must notify others, such as team members or your manager, of your progress on a task. Outlook provides a couple of ways for you to do this. The most appropriate way to send a status report is to open the task and click Send Status Report in the Manage Task group on the Task tab.

You can also attach the task to an email message or forward the task as an email message. When you're composing a message, tasks are one of the items you can select from the Attach Item list. With a task selected in the Tasks list, you can click Forward in the Respond group on the Ribbon to forward the task as an email message. Forwarding a task does not reassign it to the recipient.

Do it!

B-3:   Sending a task status report

Here's how	Here's why
1 Display the Task list	From the Navigation bar, click Tasks.
Change to Simple List view	
2 Edit the *yy*: **Update Sales Web site** task	Double-click the task assigned to you by your partner.
Set the % Complete to **25%**	You don't have to save your change yet.
3 Click **Send Status Report**	A Message window opens. The Subject line is completed for you, and details of the task are entered into the message body.
Observe the To box	Because this task was assigned to you by your partner, his or her address is already filled in. If this were a task you created, you would have to enter the recipient's address.
In the message area, enter **Change list created.**	A message is optional because the task details are already in the message body.
Press (↵ ENTER)	To move to the next line.
4 Click **Send**	To send the message to your partner.
5 Save the task	Click Save & Close.
6 From the Navigation bar, click **Mail**	To view your Inbox.
7 Select the message	

-----Original Task-----
Subject: 02: Update Sales Web Site
Priority: Normal

Start date: Tue 3/5/2013
Due date: Tue 3/26/2013

Status: In Progress
% Complete: 25%
Actual work: 0 hours

Requested by: Student01

Tracking tasks

Explanation
You might want to receive a confirmation when an assigned task is completed. You track the completion of assigned tasks by using the "Send me a status report when this task is complete" option.

To track a completed task:

1 Create a task.

2 Assign the task.

3 Check "Send me a status report when this task is complete."

4 Send the task request.

When the task is marked completed by the recipient, you'll receive an email notification.

Do it!

B-4: Tracking an assigned task

Here's how	Here's why
1 Activate Tasks	
2 In the list of tasks, check the box next to the *yy*: **Update Sales Web site** task	To mark the task as completed. Alternatively, you can open the task, change the % Complete to 100%, and save your changes.
3 Activate Mail	
Observe the Task Completed email message	-----Original Task----- **Subject:** 02: Update Sales Web Site **Priority:** Normal **Start date:** Tue 3/5/2013 **Due date:** Tue 3/26/2013 **Status:** Completed **% Complete:** 100% **Date completed:** Mon 2/18/2013 **Actual work:** 0 hours **Requested by:** Student01

Task options

Explanation

All tasks have several predefined settings, which you can modify by using the Outlook Options dialog box, shown in Exhibit 5-5. The options are described in the following table.

Option	Use to...
Set reminders on tasks with due dates	Automatically set reminders for a specified time when a task has a due date. Disabled by default.
Keep my task list updated with copies of tasks I assign to other people	Track tasks that you've assigned. Enabled by default.
Send status report when I complete an assigned task	Automatically send a status report when you complete an assigned task. Enabled by default.
Overdue task color; Completed task color	Select colors for tasks that are overdue or completed. The default colors are red (overdue) and gray (completed).
Set Quick Click flag	Set the type of flag to be used when you click in the flag column in your Inbox. By default, the flag type is set to Today.
Task working hours per day	Set your regular workday length. The default is 8 hours.
Task working hours per week	Set your regular workweek length. The default is 40 hours.

To open the Outlook Options dialog box and display the task options, click the File tab and click Options. In the left pane of the Outlook Options dialog box, click Tasks.

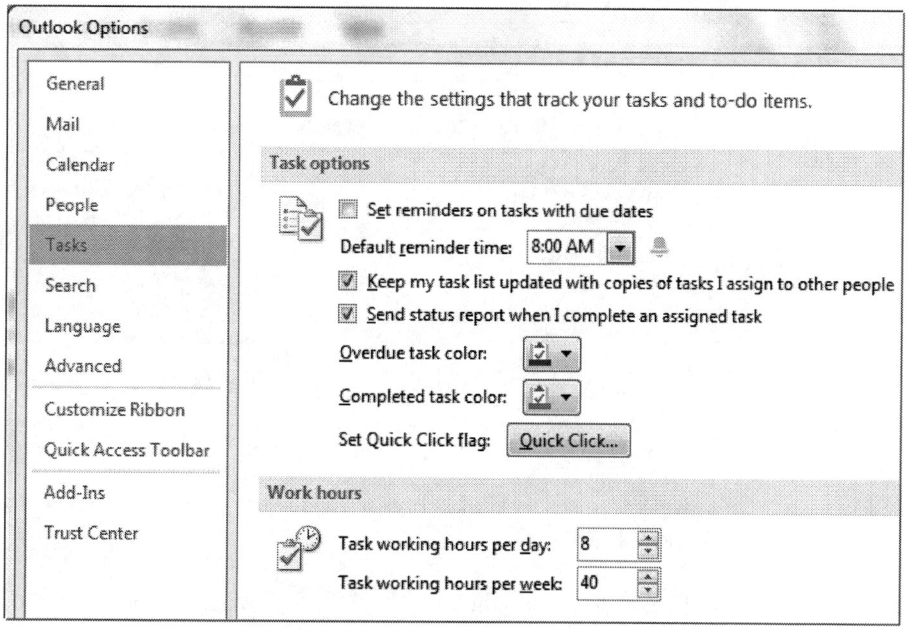

Exhibit 5-5: Task options

Do it!

B-5: Setting task options

Here's how	Here's why
1 Click the **File** tab and click **Options**	To open the Outlook Options dialog box.
In the left pane, click **Tasks**	To display the task options.
2 Observe the options	The options you set here apply to all tasks.
3 Set a new color for overdue tasks	Select any color in the box.
4 Change your daily working hours to **10**	You can select the text and enter 10, or you can use the arrows to scroll up to 10.
Change your work week to **50** hours	
5 Click **OK**	To close the dialog box and set the options.

Printing tasks

Explanation

You can print tasks just like you print messages. On the File tab, click Print, and use the print options to print one task or multiple tasks. As with messages, you can print in Table Style, which lists all tasks, or Memo Style, which prints a single task. You can also print a single task by right-clicking it in the Task list and choosing Quick Print.

Do it!

B-6: Printing tasks

Here's how	Here's why
1 Select a task	
Click the **File** tab and click **Print**	
2 Observe the print styles	You can print all tasks or just a single task.
3 Click the **Back** button	
	To return to the main Outlook window.
4 Click the **Home** tab	If necessary.
5 Right-click a task and choose **Quick Print**	To print the task with the default settings.
6 Close any open windows	Leave Outlook open.

Unit summary: Tasks

Topic A In this topic, you learned that an Outlook task is an activity that must be completed in a specified period of time. You used the **Tasks folder** and the To-Do Bar's **Task list** to add and edit a task. Next, you created a **recurring task** by specifying the recurrence pattern and the range of recurrence. You learned how to use different **Task views** and marked a task as completed.

Topic B In this topic, you **assigned** a task to another person. You also accepted, declined, and delegated **task requests**. In addition, you sent a **status report** for an assigned task. You also **tracked** the completion of an assigned task, set task options, and printed tasks.

Review questions

1 How do you create a task?

2 How can you assign a task to someone else?

3 Who is allowed to edit a task?

4 Which of the following is the term that Outlook uses to describe a task that needs to be performed on a regular basis?

   A Scheduled

   B Repeating

   C Recurring

   D Frequent

5 Name two ways to mark a task as completed.

6 True or false? When a task is marked as completed, it appears in the Tasks To-Do List view with a strikethrough line.

7 True or false? You can set the % Complete for a task only in increments of 25%.

8 When a task request is declined, who owns the task?

9 Describe the procedure for sending a status report on a task.

Independent practice activity

In this activity, you'll create a task and modify it to be a recurring task. You'll assign a task and track its completion. You'll also accept a task request and mark a task as completed.

1 Create a task with the subject *XX*: **Prepare Web usage report**, where *XX* is your partner's number. Specify the start date as the first working day of the next month, and specify the due date as 10 days after the start date.

2 Save and close the task.

3 Change the Task view to Detailed.

4 Edit the new task to make it a recurring task. Specify the Recurrence pattern as weekly. The task must recur every Wednesday.

5 Assign the task to your partner. Track the completion of the task.

6 Accept the task request from your partner. Print the task.

7 Mark the task as completed.

Unit 6

Appointments and events

Complete this unit, and you'll know how to:

A Use the Calendar to set up and view single and recurring appointments.

B Modify, delete, and restore appointments.

C Add one-time and recurring events.

D Change Calendar views, customize the Calendar, add holidays to the Calendar, and print Calendars.

Topic A: Creating and sending appointments

This topic covers the following Microsoft Office Specialist exam objectives for Outlook 2013.

#	Objective
3.2	**Create Appointments, Meetings, and Events**
3.2.1	Create calendar items
3.2.2	Create recurring calendar items
3.2.4	Create calendar items from messages
3.2.8	Change availability status
3.3	**Organize and Manage Appointments, Meetings, and Events**
3.3.1	Set calendar item importance
3.3.2	Forward calendar items
3.3.3	Configure reminders

Explanation

You can use Outlook's Calendar to set up appointments and organize your schedules. You can specify how much of your schedule you want to view at once. The Calendar consists of the Folder pane and the Calendar view, as shown in Exhibit 6-1. Month is the default view, but you can change the Calendar view to show the Day or Week. If you switch to Day view, the selected day is shown in one-hour increments, but can be changed to show smaller increments.

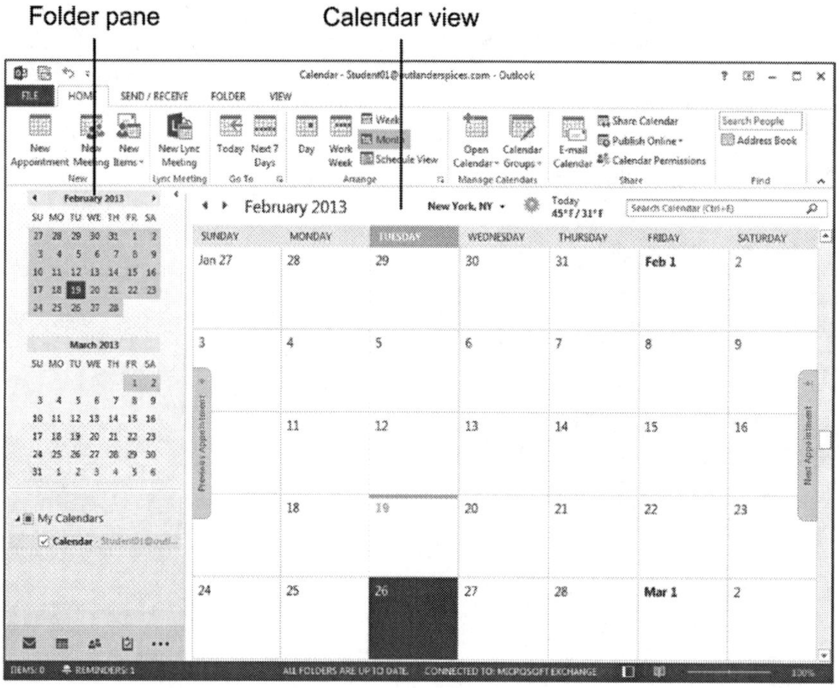

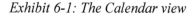

Exhibit 6-1: The Calendar view

Creating appointments

Explanation

In Outlook terminology, an *appointment* is a time slot that you reserve on your calendar. You don't invite other people to participate in an appointment. Contrast that to a *meeting*, which does involve other people.

More precisely, an appointment doesn't include any attendees who participate in your Outlook calendaring system. A meeting does involve such people. For example, a doctor appointment would be an appointment, not a meeting, because your doctor doesn't participate in your Outlook calendar, even if she uses Outlook to schedule her time. A scheduled discussion with a co-worker would be a meeting because he does use the same Outlook calendaring system to manage his time.

Appointments don't have to involve anyone other than you. Time you set aside to work on a project would be scheduled on your calendar as an appointment.

There are several ways to create an appointment:

- On the Home tab, click New Appointment.
- On the Home tab, click New Items and choose Appointment.
- From the Day or Week view, double-click the time slot during which your appointment should be scheduled. The appointment's start time will be set to the time slot you double-clicked.
- From the Day or Week view, right-click the time slot during which your appointment should be scheduled and choose New Appointment. The appointment's start time will be set to the time slot you right-clicked.

Any of the preceding methods opens the Appointment window, shown in Exhibit 6-2. Here, you specify the subject, location, time, and duration of the appointment.

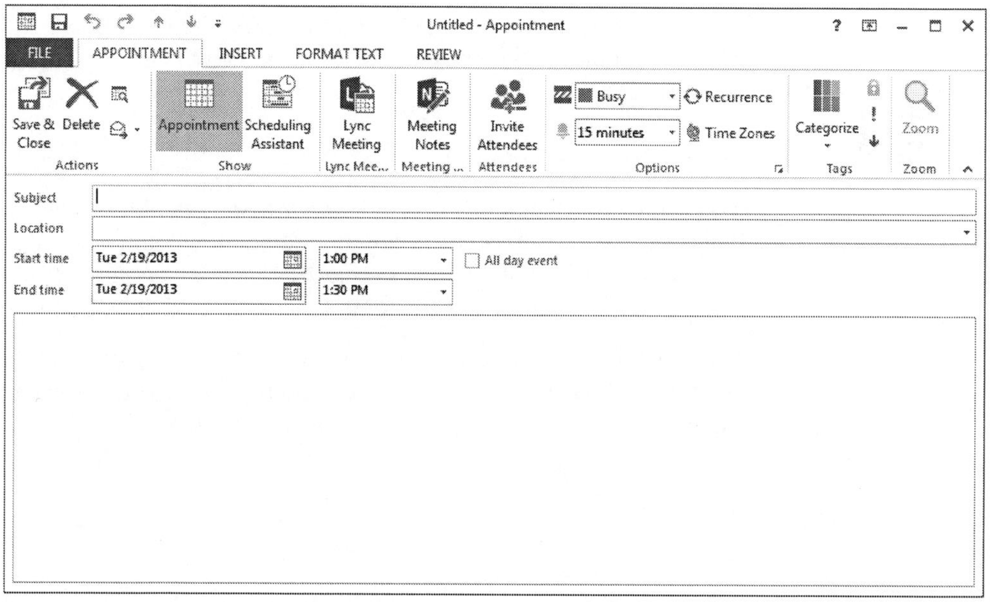

Exhibit 6-2: Creating an appointment

If you do not select a time slot before opening the Appointment window, the next available 30 minute interval is used as the Start and End times, by default. You can change the date by clicking the Calendar button and using the Date Navigator. You can also type the date into the Start time and End time fields. In addition to typing the dates, you can also type words and phrases, such as Tomorrow, Two Weeks from Today, or New Year's Day and Outlook will automatically fill in the date for you. To specify the time of day, select the Start time or End time from the list or click the All day event box for activities that require the entire day.

Keep in mind that an appointment does not include a recipient list. If you click the Invite Attendees button on the Appointment tab, you will create a meeting rather than an appointment.

You can specify several options by using the Options group on the Appointment tab. You can use the Show As list to specify your availability status, which can be Free, Working Elsewhere, Tentative, Busy, or Out of Office. Each status has a color associated with it. You can also set a reminder for the appointment. To save the appointment, click Save & Close. After you create and save an appointment, it appears in your Calendar view.

Marking an appointment as private

You can mark an appointment as private to prevent other people from accessing the details of your appointments, contacts, or tasks. To ensure that other people cannot read the items you mark as private, do not grant them Read permission to your Calendar, Contacts, or Tasks folders. To mark an appointment as private, click the lock button in the Tags group.

Setting importance for a calendar item

You can mark the importance level of calendar items as being of High Importance or Low Importance. When an email is sent for a calendar item, the Importance level appears in the message.

Forwarding appointments

You can forward an appointment to other people, and they can copy the appointment to their calendars. To forward an appointment, either right-click it in the calendar and choose Forward, or click Forward on the Calendar Tools | Appointment tab. Address the message as you would any new email message, and click Send.

If you receive a forwarded appointment, open the message and double-click the appointment. If you want to add the appointment to your calendar, click "Copy to My Calendar" in the Actions group on the Appointment tab.

Do it!   **A-1:   Setting up an appointment**

Here's how	Here's why
1 Switch to Calendar view	From the Navigation bar, click Calendar.
In the Arrange group, click **Day**	(If necessary.) To switch to Day view.
2 Click **New Appointment**	To open a new Appointment window.
3 In the Subject box, enter **Project Research**	To specify the purpose of the appointment.
4 In the Location box, enter **Research Library**	
5 From the Start time list, select tomorrow's date	To specify the start date for the appointment. By default, the end date is the same as the start date.
From the list next to the Start time list, select **10:00 AM**	To specify the start time for the appointment. The end time appears as 30 minutes from the start time.
From the list next to the End time list, select **12:00 PM**	To specify an end time two hours after the start time.
Observe the text area under the End time lists	You can enter any additional comments here.
6 From the Show As list, select **Out Of Office**	(In the Options group on the Appointment tab.) So that your calendar shows that you will be out of the office for this appointment.
7 From the Reminder list, select **30 minutes**	(In the Options group on the Appointment tab.) You'll receive audible and visual notifications 30 minutes before the appointment.
8 Click **Save & Close**	To save the appointment and close the Appointment window. The Next Appointment button in the Calendar view becomes active.
9 Click as shown	The calendar for tomorrow is shown, with the time of your appointment.

10	Right-click the **Project Research** appointment and choose **Forward**	
	Enter your partner's email address, and click **Send**	
11	When you receive the forwarded appointment message, open it	
	Double-click the appointment attachment and observe the Ribbon	You could click Copy to My Calendar if you wanted to add this appointment to your calendar. For now, though, you'll just close the appointment.
12	Close the appointment and the message from your partner	
13	Switch to the Calendar view	From the Navigation bar, click Calendar.

Adding recurring appointments

Explanation

Appointments that occur regularly are known as *recurring appointments*. For example, let's say you need to submit expenses monthly. You could schedule a recurring appointment near the end of each month to prepare your expense report.

Create a recurring appointment by using the same techniques you use to create a one-time appointment. Before saving, click Recurrence in the Options group on the Appointment tab. Specify the details of the recurrence by using the Appointment Recurrence dialog box, shown in Exhibit 6-3. Click OK to save those details, and then click Save & Close to save your appointment.

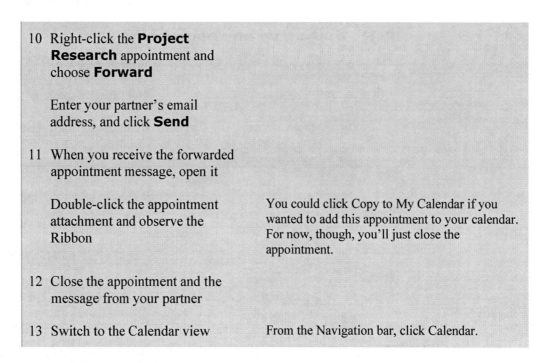

Exhibit 6-3: The Appointment Recurrence dialog box

Do it!   **A-2: Adding a recurring appointment**

Here's how	Here's why
1 Click **New Appointment**	(In Calendar view.)
2 In the Subject box, enter **Expense report**	
3 Set the Start time as the last Wednesday of the month at 3:00 PM Set the End time to 30 minutes after the start time	
4 In the Options group on the Appointment tab, click **Recurrence**	To open the Appointment Recurrence dialog box.
Observe the Start, End, and Duration boxes	You can set these values here rather than when creating the appointment.
5 Under Recurrence pattern, configure the recurrence as shown	

Recurrence pattern

- ○ Daily   ○ Day `27` of every `1` month(s)
- ○ Weekly   ● The `last` ▾ `Wednesday` ▾ of every `1` month(s)
- ● Monthly
- ○ Yearly

6 Observe the "Range of recurrence" section	You would use this portion of the dialog box to set the starting and ending dates for the recurrence.
7 Click **OK**	To close the Appointment Recurrence dialog box.
8 Click **Save & Close**	
9 On the Home tab, click **Month**	(In the Arrange group.) To switch to the monthly view of your calendar. Your recurring appointment is shown on the last Wednesday of the month.
Click the Forward arrow, as shown	 ◄ ▶ **February 2013** SUNDAY MONDAY
	To move to the next month. Your recurring appointment is also listed for this month.

Creating appointments from email messages

Explanation

You can create an appointment from an email message by dragging it to the Calendar folder. The Appointment window will open, giving you the opportunity to enter necessary details. The original message will be added as an attachment to the appointment.

For example, let's say your co-worker sends you a note about an interesting seminar and you decide to attend. Creating an appointment from the email message reduces clutter in your Inbox while keeping the message accessible in case you need to refer to it later.

There's another way to create an appointment from an email message. While previewing the message, or while it's open, click Move on the Ribbon and choose Calendar. The Appointment window will open so that you can enter necessary details.

Do it!

A-3: Creating an appointment from an email message

Here's how	Here's why
1 Switch to the Mail view	
2 Compose an email message to your partner, with these details:	

> Subject   Spice seminar
>
> I thought you might be interested in this seminar.
> It will be held next Tuesday at the XYZ University Auditorium.
>
> ### History of Spices
> By Dr. Basil Rosemary
>
> Uncover hidden facts and the rich details of spices and their impacts on the early development of society.

Send the message	
3 When your partner's message arrives in your Inbox, open or preview it	It might take a moment to arrive in your Inbox.
4 On the Ribbon, click **Move** and choose **Other Folder...**	
Select **Calendar** and click **OK**	An Appointment window opens. The subject line is filled in and the email message is attached. You'll need to enter the other details.
5 In the Location box, enter **XYZ University Auditorium**	

6 Enter next Tuesday at **9:00 AM**
   as the Start time

   Enter **11:30 AM** as the End time

7 Click **Save & Close**

8 Observe your Inbox   The email message is gone.

9 View next week on your Calendar   The seminar is listed for next Tuesday.

10 Double-click the   To open it.
   Spice Seminar appointment

   Double-click the attachment   Outlook has not deleted the original email
                                         message, but has attached it to the appointment
                                         record.

   Close the Message and   To return to the Calendar.
   Appointment windows

Topic B: Modifying appointments

This topic covers the following Microsoft Office Specialist exam objectives for Outlook 2013.

#	Objective
3.2	**Create Appointments, Meetings, and Events**
3.2.3	Cancel calendar items
3.3	**Organize and Manage Appointments, Meetings, and Events**
3.3.6	Update calendar items

Explanation

After you create an appointment, you might need to reschedule or cancel it. You can cancel an appointment by deleting it. You can also restore a deleted appointment.

Rescheduling appointments

You can reschedule an appointment by changing the date, time, location, or other details. To edit an appointment:

1 Double-click the appointment to open it.

2 Make the necessary changes.

3 Click Save & Close.

You can also reschedule appointments by dragging them. With this method, it's easiest to change the date of an appointment in Month view. To drag an appointment to a new time on the same day, use Day view.

Do it!

B-1: Editing an appointment's text

Here's how	Here's why
1 Display the calendar in Month view	(From the Home tab, click Month.) You're going to reschedule the Project Research appointment.
On the Home tab, click **Today**	In the Go To group.
2 Double-click the **Project Research** appointment	(In the calendar grid.) To open the Appointment window.
3 Change the start date and the end date to one day later	To postpone the appointment by one day.
Edit the Location box to read **Research Library, Building K**	
4 In the text area, type the indicated text	1. Spice origins 2. Trade agreements with Malaysia
5 Save the appointment	The appointment is postponed by one day.
6 Point to the appointment	

Project Research

Start: 2/21/2013   10:00 AM
End: 2/21/2013   12:00 PM

Location: Research Library, Building K
Reminder: 30 minutes

21

10:00am Project Research; Research Library, Building K

28

The pop-up shows details of the appointment.

7 Drag the appointment back to its original day	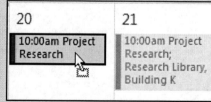

You can change the date of an appointment by dragging it in Month view.

8 Change to Day view	Click Day on the Ribbon.
9 Drag the appointment so it starts at 11:00 AM	You can change the time of an appointment by dragging it in Day view.

Rescheduling recurring appointments

Explanation   If you want to modify a recurring appointment, here's how:

1 Double-click the appointment to open the Open Recurring Item dialog box.
2 If you want to modify a single occurrence, select "Just this one." If you want to modify all occurrences of the recurring appointment, select "The entire series."
3 Click OK to open the Appointment window.
4 Click Recurrence in the Options group on the Appointment tab.
5 Make the necessary changes and click OK.
6 Click Save & Close.

Do it!   ## B-2:   Modifying a recurring appointment

Here's how	Here's why
1 Switch to Month view	
2 Double-click the **Expense Report** appointment	To display the Open Recurring Item dialog box. You can modify either the selected occurrence or all occurrences of the recurring appointment.
3 Select **The entire series**	You'll change all occurrences of this recurring appointment.
Click **OK**	To open the Appointment Series window.
4 Click **Recurrence**	(In the Options group on the Appointment Series tab.) To open the Appointment Recurrence dialog box.
Under Appointment time, from the Start list, select **11:30 AM**	
Change the appointment to occur on the last Monday of every month, as shown	
⦿ The [last ▼] [Monday ▼] of every [1] month(s)	
Under "Range of recurrence," set the start date to today's date	For a recurring appointment, the range does not need to begin on the date of the first appointment.
Click **OK**	
5 Save and close the appointment	
6 Observe the calendar	(In Month view.) The appointment has moved to the last Monday of the month. If today is after the last Monday of the month, the event will not be visible. You'll have to view the next month to see it.

Deleting and restoring appointments

Explanation   You can delete appointments that are no longer needed or that have been canceled. To delete an appointment, select it and click the Delete button on the Ribbon. You can also press the Delete key or press Ctrl+D.

You can restore a deleted appointment. If you haven't done anything else since deleting the appointment, you can press Ctrl+Z to undo the deletion. Until you empty the Deleted Items folder, you can restore the appointment from there. You can drag it back to the Calendar folder, or right-click the item and choose Move, Calendar.

Do it!   ## B-3: Deleting and restoring an appointment

Here's how	Here's why
1 On the Home tab, click **Today**	If necessary, to return to this month and highlight today's date on the calendar.
2 Select the **Project Research** appointment	You'll delete this appointment.
3 Click **Delete**	![Delete button] To delete the appointment.
4 Press (CTRL) + (Z)	To undo the deletion.
5 Select the **Project Research** appointment	You'll delete this appointment again.
6 Press (DELETE)	
7 Click ...	(From the Navigation bar.) To display the Navigation menu.
8 Click **Folders**	To display the folder list at the bottom of the Folder pane.
Select **Deleted Items**	
9 Right-click the **Project Research** appointment	Student01 Project Research 10:53 AM In the folder list.
Click **Move** and choose **Calendar**	To move the item back to the Calendar.
10 Activate the Calendar	The appointment has been restored.
11 Delete the Project Research appointment	Select it, and then either click Delete or press the Delete key.

Topic C: Working with events

This topic covers the following Microsoft Office Specialist exam objectives for Outlook 2013.

#	Objective
3.2	**Create Appointments, Meetings, and Events**
3.2.1	Create calendar items
3.2.2	Create recurring calendar items

Explanation

In Outlook, an *event* is an activity that lasts for a period of one or more days and that can be added to the Calendar. There are three types of events in Outlook: single-day, multi-day, and recurring. For example, workshops, conferences, and seminars can be single- or multi-day events. Birthdays and anniversaries are examples of events that recur annually. Quarterly tax filing deadlines are an example of events that recur on something other than an annual basis. By default, Outlook assumes that events last for at least one day. However, you can change this setting and specify the duration of an event.

Single- and multi-day events

You can add single-day and multi-day events to the Calendar. Here's how:

1 On the Home tab, in the New group, click New Items and choose All Day Event to open a new Event window. (You can also create an appointment and check the "All day event" box, next to the End times boxes, in the Appointment window.)

2 Specify the subject and location for the event.

3 Do one of the following:

  • If it is a single-day event that runs for the entire day, select the same date for the start and end dates. "All day event" is checked by default.

  • If it is a multi-day event, select the start and end dates.

4 From the Show As list on the Event tab, select the status you want shown on your Calendar. For birthday or anniversary events, you should select Free. The other status types would be more appropriate for classes, seminars, and trips.

5 Use the Reminder list on the Event tab to specify when you want to be reminded about the event.

6 Click Save & Close to save the event and close the Event window.

Marking an event as private

You can mark an event as private to prevent other people from accessing the details of your personal events. To mark an event as private, open it and click Private in the Options group on the Event tab.

Creating events from messages and tasks

You can also create events from messages and tasks. To do so, drag the email message or task to the Calendar folder. The Appointment window will open. Enter the necessary details and click Save & Close.

Do it!   ## C-1: Adding an event

Here's how	Here's why
1 Switch to Month view	If necessary.
2 Click **New Items** and choose **All Day Event**	(In the New group on the Home tab.) To open a new Event window.
3 In the Subject box, enter **Medicinal spice seminar**	
4 Specify the start date as the first Monday of the next month	Use the Date Navigator to advance to the next month.
5 Specify the end date as the date that is two working days after the start date	
6 From the Show As list, select **Out of Office**	
Observe the Reminder list	The default reminder is set for 18 hours before the event.
7 Click **Save & Close**	To save the event and close the Event window.
8 View the first Monday of next month	<table><tr><td>4</td><td>5</td><td>6</td></tr><tr><td colspan="3">Medicinal spice seminar</td></tr></table>
	(Advance to the next month and view the first Monday.) The event appears as a banner across the scheduled days.

Recurring events

Explanation

Recurring events happen more than once. For example, a birthday happens every year on the same day. Estimated taxes are due every quarter. You create a recurring event by specifying a Recurrence. Here's one way to do this:

1 With the Calendar open, click New Items on the Home tab and choose All Day Event.
2 Enter the event details, such as subject, location, and date.
3 Click Recurrence (in the Options group on the Event tab) to open the Appointment Recurrence dialog box.
4 Under Recurrence pattern, specify when and for how long the event recurs.
5 Click OK.
6 Click Save & Close.

Alternatively, you can:

1 Right-click the appropriate time slot and choose New Recurring Event. For example, in Month view, right-click a day's box to create a recurring event on that date. Both the Event window and the Appointment Recurrence dialog box open.
2 Define the recurrence pattern and click OK.
3 Enter the event details, such as subject, location, and so forth.
4 Click Save & Close.

Do it!

C-2: Adding an annual event

Here's how	Here's why
1 Click **New Items** and choose **All Day Event**	(In the New group on the Home tab.) To open a new Event window.
Specify the subject as **National Ice Cream Day**	
2 For the Start time, select the third Sunday in July	Depending on the current date, you might notice a message in the InfoBar, telling you that the selected date occurs in the past. Because this event will be changed to an annual one, you can ignore this message.
3 On the Event tab, click **Recurrence**	(From the Options group.) To open the Appointment Recurrence dialog box.
Under Recurrence pattern, select **Yearly**	

4 Verify that the recurrence period
   is selected as shown

Recur every	1	year(s)				
○ On:	July ▼	21				
◉ On the:	third ▼	Sunday ▼	of	July ▼		

5 Close the Appointment
   Recurrence dialog box

6 Save the event

7 Switch to Month view   If necessary.

8 Navigate to July

21

National Ice
Cream Day

(Use the Date Navigator or the Forward button.)
The event appears on the third Sunday.

9 Press CTRL + G   To open the Go To Date dialog box.

   In the Date box, enter   Where 20## is next year, such as 7/1/2014.
   7/1/20##

   Confirm that **Month Calendar**
   is selected

   Click **OK**   Next year's July is shown. National Ice Cream
                                        Day is shown on the third Sunday.

10 Click **Today**   (On the Ribbon.) To display the current date in
                                        Calendar view.

Topic D: Using Calendar Views

This topic covers the following Microsoft Office Specialist exam objectives for Outlook 2013.

#	Objective
1.3	**Print and Save Information in Outlook**
1.3.2	Print calendars
3.1	**Create and Manage Calendars**
3.1.1	Adjust viewing details for calendars
3.1.2	Modify calendar time zones
3.1.4	Demonstrate how to set calendar work times

Explanation

Outlook provides various Calendar views, including Day, Work Week, Week, Month, and Schedule. To change the view, click the appropriate button on the Ribbon. (Buttons for these views are on the Home tab and the View tab.) You can view as much of your schedule as you want to at a time.

Day view

Day view, as shown in Exhibit 6-4, shows all of your calendar items for a single day. The current date is selected by default. If you want to view items for another day, click the Forward or Back navigation buttons to the left of the date or use the Date Navigator in the Folder pane.

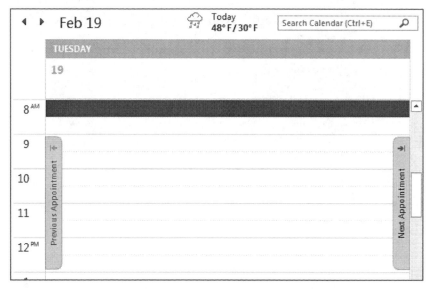

Exhibit 6-4: Day view

Work Week and Week views

Work Week view displays the current five-day work week, as shown in Exhibit 6-5. If you prefer to view a full seven-day week, click Week to show Week view. Use the Forward and Back buttons to view other weeks, or click a date in the Date Navigator to show that week's items.

Exhibit 6-5: Work Week view

Month view

Month view, shown in Exhibit 6-6, shows the entire month. The heading of today's date is highlighted in blue. The box for the date you have selected is shaded in dark blue. Dates in the previous and next months are displayed so that there are no empty boxes in the calendar.

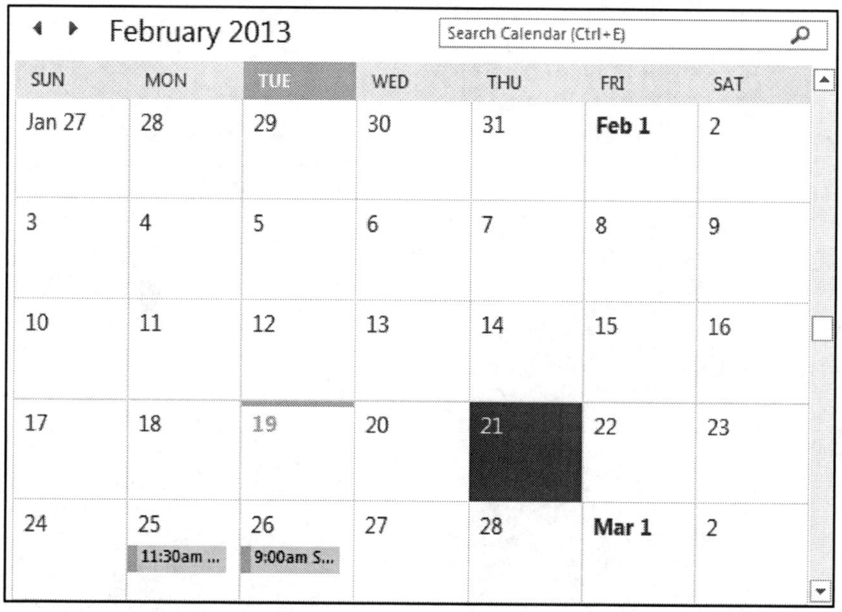

Exhibit 6-6: Month view

Schedule view

Schedule view, shown in Exhibit 6-7, is a combined view of all of the calendars you have opened. This view is useful for checking the availability of the members on a team or in a workgroup.

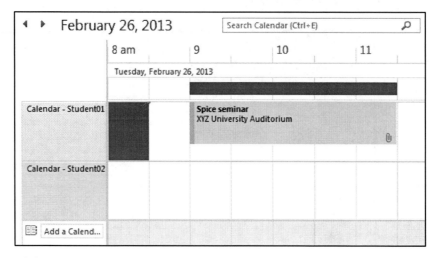

Exhibit 6-7: Schedule view

Calendar weather bar

From Calendar view, you can observe the weather for a particular city, directly from Outlook's calendar. Depending on screen size, up to a three-day forecast is visible. In addition, you can customize the Weather bar to show forecasts for up to five cities.

Do it!

D-1:   Exploring Calendar views

Here's how	Here's why
1 On the Home tab, click **Day**	To switch to Day view.
2 Observe the Calendar view	Day view shows the day's calendar items.
3 Click **Work Week**	(On the Home tab.) The calendar grid displays the current work week, Monday to Friday. Use this view to see the entire work week at a glance.
4 Click **Week**	To show the full seven-day week. Weekend days are shaded gray.
5 Click **Month**	To view the calendar for the entire month.
6 Click **Schedule View**	To show today's calendar in Schedule view. If you had multiple calendars open, such as those of a co-worker, you'd see events from all of the calendars listed in this single view.
7 Click **Day**	To return to the default view.
8 Observe the Weather bar	At the top of the Day view. The current conditions and local forecast are visible.

Setting workdays and times

Explanation

The default work week is Monday through Friday, and the work day typically begins at 8:00 AM and ends at 5:00 PM. You might want to change the work days or the times of the day. You can change these calendar settings by using the Calendar page in the Outlook Options dialog box, shown in Exhibit 6-8.

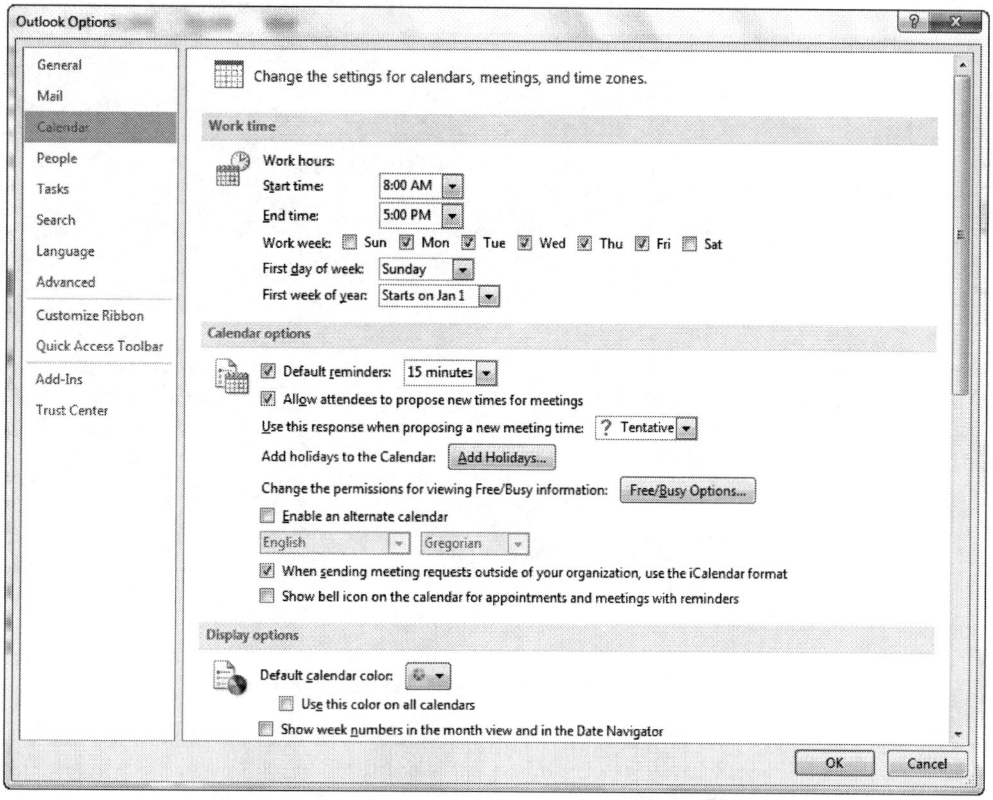

Exhibit 6-8: Calendar settings in the Outlook Options dialog box

D-2: Setting Calendar options

Here's how	Here's why
1 Click the **File** tab and then click **Options**	To open the Outlook Options dialog box.
In the left pane, click **Calendar**	To display Calendar-related options.
2 Under Work hours, change the Start time to **9:00 AM**	To change the work week's start time.
Change the End time to **6:00 PM**	
3 From the "First day of week" list, select **Monday**	To switch to a Monday-to-Sunday week.
4 Click **OK**	To close the Outlook Options dialog box.
5 Switch to Day view	The day now starts at 9:00 AM (the 8:00 AM time slot is shaded gray).
6 Switch to Week view	The week runs from Monday to Sunday.
7 Switch to Month view	The first column is now Monday, not Sunday.

Displaying multiple time zones

You might have business associates or clients who are located around the world. When scheduling activities such as conference calls, you need to consider the time zones for these locations. You can add time zones to schedule your activities more easily.

To display a second time zone:

1 On the File tab, click Options to open the Outlook Options dialog box.

2 In the left pane, click Calendar.

3 In the Time zones section, check "Show a second time zone."

4 (Optional) Enter a label. If you do so, it will be displayed in Day view and other locations where times are displayed.

5 From the Time zone list, select the time zone you want to add.

6 Check or clear "Automatically adjust for daylight savings time" to match the practices of your new locale. (Not all regions observe Daylight Savings Time.)

7 Click OK.

Do it!   **D-3:   Displaying multiple time zones**

Here's how	**Here's why**
1 Open the Outlook Options dialog box	Click the File tab and click Options.
In the left pane, click **Calendar**	To display Calendar-related options.
2 Under Time zones, check **Show a second time zone**	Scroll down to find this section.
From the second Time zone list, select a time zone other than your local one	For example, if you're in the Eastern time zone, choose the Pacific time zone.
In the Label box, enter **There**	
3 Under Time zones, in the first Label box, enter **Here**	You are using these labels to distinguish between your local and second time zones. At your office, you might use more precise labels, such as Eastern, Mtn, or PST.
4 Click **OK**	To save your changes.
5 Switch to Day view	

There	Here	
5^{AM}	8^{AM}	
6	9	
7	10	
8	11	

Both time zones are displayed in Day view, with your local time zone to the right of the secondary time zone.

Holidays

Explanation

You can display holidays commonly celebrated in your country in the Calendar. Holidays appear on the Calendar as all-day events.

To add the holidays to the Calendar:

1 Open the Outlook Options dialog box, and click Calendar.
2 Under Calendar options, click Add Holidays to open the Add Holidays to Calendar dialog box.
3 In the list of countries, check your country.
4 Click OK. A message states that the holidays are added to your Calendar.
5 Click OK to return to the Outlook Options dialog box.
6 Click OK to close the Outlook Options dialog box.

◄ ► February 2013		New York, NY ▾	Today 48° F / 30° F	Search Calendar (Ctrl+E)		
MONDAY	TUESDAY	WEDNESDAY	THURSDAY	FRIDAY	SATURDAY	SUNDAY
Jan 28	29	30	31	Feb 1	2 Groundhog Day; United States	3
4	5	6	7	8	9	10
11	12	13	14 Valentine's Day; United States	15	16	17
18 Presidents' Day; United States	19	20	21	22	23	24
25 11:30am Expense report	26 9:00am Spice seminar; XYZ University Aud...	27	28	Mar 1	2	3

Exhibit 6-9: Month view in the Calendar, showing holidays

Do it!   **D-4:   Adding holidays to the Calendar**

Here's how	Here's why
1 Open the Outlook Options dialog box	
Click **Calendar**	To display Calendar-related options.
2 Under Calendar options, click **Add Holidays**	To open the Add Holidays to Calendar dialog box.
3 Verify that your country is checked	
4 Click **OK**	To import the holidays into your Calendar. A message states that the holidays have been added.
Click **OK**	To return to the Outlook Options dialog box.
5 Click **OK**	To return to the Calendar.
6 Switch to Month view	Holidays are now listed on your Calendar. If no official holidays fall in the current month, view another month.

Printing calendars

Explanation

There might be times when you want a hard copy of your calendar, such as when you're going to be away from the office and don't have access to your computer. To print your calendar, display the calendar you want to print, click the File tab, and then click Print.

You can print your calendar using one of the following styles:

- **Daily Style** — Prints the daily schedule and includes the daily task list and a section for notes.
- **Weekly Agenda Style** — Includes seven days with a box for each day, with smaller boxes for weekend days. Also includes small versions of the current and next months.
- **Weekly Calendar Style** — Includes all seven days in columns, with hours as rows.
- **Monthly Style** — Prints one full month in a traditional calendar layout.
- **Tri-fold Style** — Prints three "panes": one for today's schedule, one for tasks, and another for the week at a glance.
- **Calendar Details Style** — Prints a list of appointments by day.

To print a calendar, in one of the Calendar views, click the File tab and then click Print. Select the style you want, and click Print.

To print a single appointment, open it, click the File tab, and click Print. To print the appointment and its details in Memo Style, click the Print button. You can also right-click the appointment in the calendar and choose Quick Print.

Do it!

D-5: Printing a Calendar

Here's how	Here's why
1 Click the **File** tab and click **Print**	To display printing options for the Calendar.
Observe the settings	Because you are in Month view, Monthly Style is the default choice.
2 Select **Daily Style** and observe the preview	It lists today's appointments.
Note the page indicator at the bottom of the preview pane	◀ 1 of 35 ▶
	The entire month will print in Daily Style. Like any document, you can print just single pages.
3 Select **Monthly Style** and click **Print**	To print one month of your calendar.
4 Right-click an appointment and choose **Quick Print**	To print a single appointment.
5 Close any open windows	

Unit summary: Appointments and events

Topic A In this topic, you learned about the **Calendar** view. You added **appointments** by using the Appointment window. You added a recurring appointment, and you learned how to add an appointment from a message.

Topic B In this topic, you **edited** a regular appointment and a recurring appointment. Then you **deleted** an appointment and **restored** the deleted appointment.

Topic C In this topic, you added **events** to the Calendar. You added both one-time and recurring events.

Topic D In this topic, you compared the various Calendar views. You changed the **work-day times** and added a **second time zone** to your Calendar. Then you added a holiday to your Calendar and printed a Calendar.

Review questions

1 Which of the following can be used to display a different month? [Choose all that apply.]

A The Forward and Back navigation buttons in Month view

B The Current View list

C The Date Navigator

D The Daily Task list

2 What is the difference between an appointment, a meeting, and an event?

3 What is the definition of a recurring appointment?

4 How do you create a recurring appointment?

5 Which button can you use to quickly display the appointments for the current day?

6 What is the procedure to change your calendar so that every day starts at 9:00 AM?

7 You want to add an item to your calendar to mark the date your company was founded. Would you add a meeting, an appointment, or an event?

8 How many days are shown in the default Week view?

9 True or false? When you create an appointment from an email message, you can delete the message so that it doesn't remain in your Inbox.

10 If you delete an appointment and then find that you still need it, how do you restore it to the Calendar?

Independent practice activity

In this activity, you'll create a recurring appointment. You'll view an appointment, delete it, and restore it. In addition, you'll email an appointment and create an annual event.

1 Create an appointment for tomorrow at 9:00 AM. Specify the subject as **Spice Seminar**, the location as **Paradise Theater**, and the end time as 10:30 AM.

2 Change the appointment so that it's recurring, repeating every month for four months. (*Hint:* Under "Range of recurrence," enter the relevant value in the End after box.)

3 Observe the appointment in the various Calendar views. Print the appointment.

4 Delete all occurrences of the Spice Seminar appointment that you scheduled.

5 Set the work day to begin at 8:00 AM and end at 5:00 PM. Set the calendar week to begin on Sunday.

6 Show only a single time zone on your calendar. Remove the label for your local time zone.

Unit 7

Meeting requests and responses

Complete this unit, and you'll know how to:

A Use the Calendar to create and send meeting requests, and respond to meeting requests by accepting or declining them or by proposing a new meeting time.

B Reserve resources, manage meeting responses, and update and cancel meetings.

Topic A: Scheduling meetings

This topic covers the following Microsoft Office Specialist exam objectives for Outlook 2013.

#	Objective
3.1	**Create and Manage Calendars**
3.1.3	Delete calendars
3.1.5	Create multiple calendars
3.1.7	Overlay calendars
3.2	**Create Appointments, Meetings, and Events**
3.2.7	Use the scheduling assistant
3.3	**Organize and Manage Appointments, Meetings, and Events**
3.3.5	Respond to invitations

Explanation

In Outlook terminology, a *meeting* is a time slot you reserve on your Calendar, as well as on the Outlook Calendar of one or more additional attendees. Contrast that to an *appointment*, which does not involve other people (or involves only people who are not part of your Outlook calendaring system).

For example, if you and your co-worker Sally use Outlook's Calendar tools to coordinate a time to discuss a project, you are creating a meeting. If you schedule a time on your Calendar to visit the dentist, that's an appointment. Even though that time slot involves another person, it's not a meeting because your dentist doesn't use the same Outlook calendaring system to manage his time.

Meeting requests

A *meeting request* is a special type of message that contains all the details of a proposed meeting time. After you create a meeting request, it is sent to all of the participants you invite. Each of them can accept, decline, or suggest an alternate time for the meeting. If your Exchange environment has been set up for it, meeting requests can even book locations and equipment, such as a projector, computer, and so forth.

Calendaring is such an integral part of Outlook that the program provides many ways to create meeting requests. You will probably find one or two methods you use most often. Even if you don't use them all, it's nice to know that you can create meeting requests by using any of these methods:

- Open the Meeting window and enter the meeting details. You can open a new Meeting window in various ways:
  - In any view (Inbox, Contacts, and so forth), click New Items and choose Meeting.
  - In any Calendar view, click the New Meeting button on the Ribbon.
  - In any Calendar view, right-click a time slot and choose New Meeting Request.
  - In any view, press Ctrl+Shift+Q.

- Create an appointment or event, and then click Invite Attendees on the Ribbon. This converts the appointment or event into a meeting.
- Create an appointment or event, and then click Scheduling Assistant on the Ribbon. Add the calendars of all prospective attendees. Double-click the header atop the time slot that is free for all attendees. This converts the appointment or event into a meeting.
- In the Calendar, switch to Schedule view. Add the calendars of all prospective attendees. Double-click the header atop the time slot that is free for all attendees.
- Use drag-and-drop or the menus to move an email message to the Calendar. Using the resulting Appointment window, invite attendees; this converts the appointment into a meeting.

Exhibit 7-1: Create meeting requests in the Meeting window

Response options

To configure response options, click Response Options in the Attendees group on the Ribbon. By default, both options—Request Responses and Allow New Time Proposals—are enabled. To disable one of the options, select it to uncheck it.

Do it!

A-1: Creating and sending a meeting request

Here's how	Here's why
1 With your partner, decide who will be partner A and who will be partner B	Partner A will schedule appointments, events, and meetings at the times printed in the book. Partner B will schedule items at one hour *after* the times printed in the book.
2 Activate the Calendar	From the Navigation bar, click Calendar.
3 Click **New Meeting**	To open a new Meeting window. The InfoBar tells you that invitations have not been sent for the meeting.

4 In the To box, enter your partner's email address

In the Subject box, enter **XX: Sales strategy for the Midwest region**

In place of *XX*, use your partner's number.

In the Location box, enter **Conference Room**

To specify the location for the meeting.

5 Use the Start time and End time fields to schedule the meeting for tomorrow from **9:00 AM** to **10:00 AM**

If you're partner B, schedule the meeting for 10:00 AM to 11:00 AM.

6 Observe the Reminder list

(In the Options group on the Meeting tab.) It is set to remind you 15 minutes before the meeting.

In the Show As list, verify that **Busy** is selected

To mark the allocated time as busy in your Calendar. Other options are Free, Working Elsewhere, Tentative, and Out of Office.

7 Click **Response Options**

In the Attendees group.

Observe the settings

You can see that you are requesting responses and allowing proposals for a new time. Both settings are enabled by default.

8 Click **Send**

To send the meeting request and close the Meeting window.

9 Switch to Day view

If necessary.

View tomorrow's schedule

(Click the Forward button or click tomorrow's date in the Date Navigator.) The meeting is listed on your Calendar. Your partner's meeting will also be listed (though perhaps not immediately) because he or she invited you.

| 9 | **02: Sales strategy for the Midwest region**
Conference room
Student01 |
| 10 | 01: Sales strategy for the Midwest region
Conference Room
Student02 |

Meeting requests

Explanation

Meeting requests are delivered to all invitees, and the requests show up in the Inbox just like email messages do. When you preview or open the meeting request, you will be able to see all of the meeting's details, such as the date, time, and location. The meeting request also shows you the relevant portion of your calendar so you can quickly determine whether you can attend the meeting. This feature is shown in Exhibit 7-2.

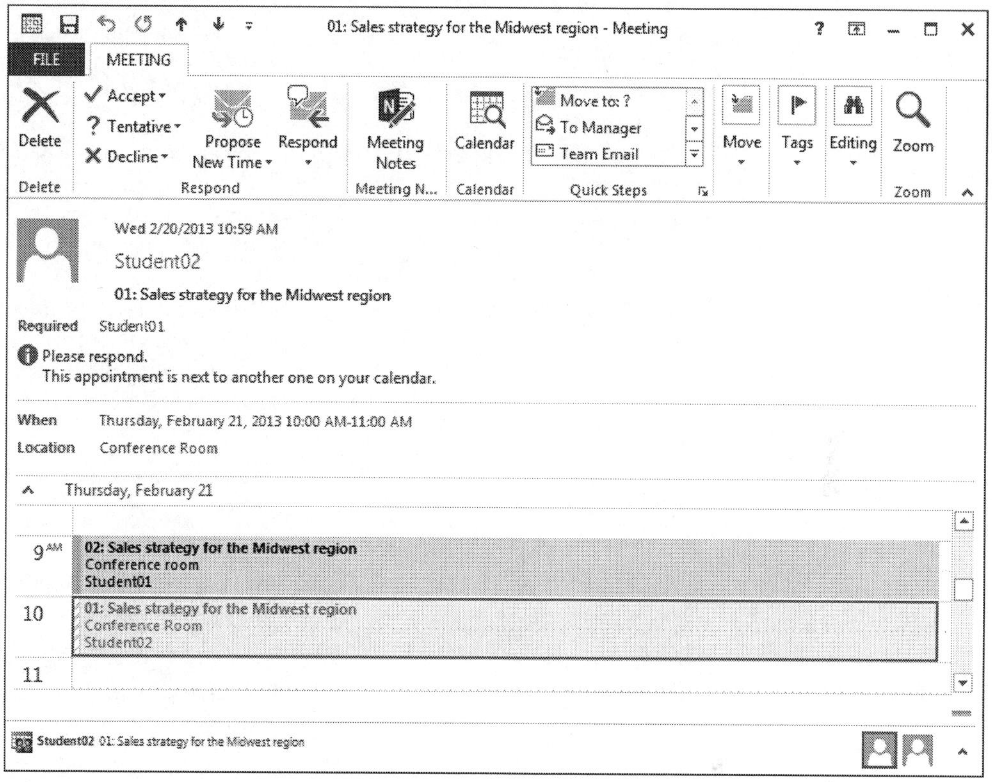

Exhibit 7-2: A Meeting Request window

Outlook provides buttons to enable you to reply to a meeting request. You can click Accept, Tentative, Decline, or Propose New Time. If you need to communicate with the meeting organizer, you can click Respond and choose Reply, Reply to All, and so forth. Doing so enables you to send an email message, such as to confirm missing details, without yet accepting or declining the request.

Depending on the action you take, Outlook will update your calendar, as well as the calendar of the organizer. For example, clicking Accept will add a meeting item to your calendar and mark you as attending in the organizer's view of the meeting.

Do it!

A-2: Reading and accepting a meeting request

Here's how	Here's why
1 Activate Mail	
Observe the new message	Student02 🔔 📧 01: Sales strategy for the Midwest re... 10:59 AM In the Message list, the icon to the right on the new message indicates that the message is a meeting request.
2 Select the *YY: Sales strategy for the Midwest region* message	When you preview or open the Meeting window, you have access to additional buttons for checking your calendar, forwarding the request, or deleting it.
Click **Calendar Preview**	(If necessary.) To show a preview of your calendar in the message body. It shows your current schedule for the date and time of this meeting request.
Observe the buttons at the top of the preview	
✔ Accept ▾ ❓ Tentative ▾ ✖ Decline ▾ 🗓 Propose New Time ▾	
3 Click **Accept**	You're given the choice to edit your response, send the response, or accept the meeting request without sending a response.
Choose **Send the Response Now**	The meeting is added to your calendar, and the request is removed from your Inbox.
4 Observe your Inbox	Student02 📅 Accepted: 02: Sales strategy for the ... 11:22 AM After a moment or two, a meeting acceptance notice from your partner will arrive.
5 Open the message	Accepted Student02 Tentative No attendees have tentatively accepted. Declined No attendees have declined. The message header indicates that your partner has accepted your request for a meeting.
6 Close the Meeting Response window	

Displaying and hiding calendars

Explanation

If you need to regularly schedule meetings with a small group of co-workers, you can add their calendars to your Calendar folder. (In fact, for Schedule view to be useful, you must first add the other attendees' calendars to your Calendar folder. Otherwise, Schedule view shows just your calendar.) You won't be able to modify the added calendars, but you'll be able to see your co-workers' availability and use Schedule view to create meeting requests for times that you see are free for all attendees.

To add a calendar:

1   In any Calendar view, click Open Calendar on the Ribbon and choose the appropriate source. For example, to open the calendar of another user within your Exchange organization, choose From Address Book.

2   Select the calendar or calendars you want to add.

3   Click Calendar.

4   Click OK.

Once you've added a calendar, it will be displayed alongside your calendar in the various views. You can also overlay the open calendars into a single view by clicking the View in Overlay Mode button on the tab for the other user's calendar. The calendars are combined into one calendar and are transparently stacked on top of one another. To no longer view the calendars in overlay mode, click the View in Side-by-Side Mode button to view the calendar alongside yours.

To hide a calendar, click the Close button (the ×) on the tab beside the other user's calendar, or uncheck the box next to that person's calendar in the Folder pane. Doing this does not remove your connection to that person's calendar; it just hides the calendar temporarily. Simply check the box in the Folder pane to show the calendar again.

To remove a calendar, right-click it in the Folder pane and choose Delete Calendar.

Viewing other users' calendars and adding them to your Calendar view requires an Exchange Server or third-party components.

A-3: Displaying and hiding calendars

Here's how	Here's why
1 Activate the Calendar	
2 In the Manage Calendars group, click **Open Calendar**	On the Ribbon.
Choose **From Address Book...**	
3 Select your partner	
Click **Calendar ->**	
Click **OK**	You can now see both calendars. Notice the changes in the Folder pane: both calendars are listed there now.
4 Switch to Day view	If necessary. You see both calendars in a tabbed arrangement.
5 Click as shown	To overlay the two calendars on the same Day view.
6 Next to your partner's name, click the **X**	To close your partner's calendar.
Observe the Folder pane	Your partner's calendar is still listed, but it's unchecked. You have not removed it, but simply hidden it from view.
7 In the Folder pane, right-click your partner's calendar and choose **Delete Calendar**	It is removed from your Folder pane. The group, Shared Calendars, remains.
8 Right-click **Shared Calendars** and choose **Delete Group**	
Click **Yes**	To delete the entire group. If it contained calendars, they would also be removed.

Scheduling meetings

Explanation

Outlook provides tools you can use to check an attendee's schedule before you create your meeting request. You can do this in Schedule view in the Calendar or in the Invite Attendees window.

When you need to regularly schedule meetings with an individual, you will probably want to add his or her calendar to your Calendar folder. For those other people with whom you don't regularly schedule meetings, you can use the Scheduling Assistant to check their calendars while scheduling a meeting. Here's how:

1 Open a new Meeting window.

2 Enter pertinent details, such as the subject, location, and date and time.

3 Optionally, enter the attendees in the To box.

4 Click Scheduling Assistant.

5 If you did not add attendees in step 3, then under the All Attendees column, click "Click here to add a name." Enter the attendee's name or email address and press Enter.

6 Highlight a suitable time that is free for all attendees. You can click a column header to select a half-hour block, or drag across multiple columns to schedule longer meetings. Use the Date Navigator to quickly scroll to future dates.

7 Click Send.

You should enter the meeting details, such as the subject, before opening the Scheduling Assistant. But if you open it before entering the details, simply click the Appointment button to return to the Meeting window.

The Scheduling Assistant requires an Exchange Server or third-party components.

A-4: Scheduling a meeting

Here's how	Here's why
1 Click **New Meeting**	
2 Enter your partner's email address in the To box	
In the Subject box, enter *XX*: **Product Planning**	Where *XX* is your partner's lab number.
In the Location box, enter **Conference Room**	You must enter meeting details before opening the Scheduling Assistant.
3 Click **Scheduling Assistant**	
	To open the Scheduling Assistant. Because you entered your partner's email address, his or her calendar is made available in the Assistant. You could add others.
4 Scroll to show tomorrow's schedule	You have already scheduled a meeting with your partner for tomorrow morning at 9:00. This time is blocked out on the schedule.
5 Click where indicated	
	(On the gray heading under 1:00 PM tomorrow.) To select the 1:00-to-1:30 PM half-hour slot.
6 Click again in the same spot and drag to the right	
	To select the whole 1:00 hour.
7 Click **Send**	
	To send the meeting request to your partner.
8 View tomorrow's schedule in Day view	
	The newly proposed meeting is shown.

Declining meeting requests

Explanation

If you have a conflict—perhaps you forgot to update your calendar with a prior commitment—you can decline a meeting request. When you do so, the organizer receives a message saying that you have declined the meeting request. Declined meeting requests will not be added to your calendar.

Canceling meetings

You can cancel a meeting if you were the organizer of it. Select it on your calendar and click Cancel Meeting on the Ribbon.

If all of the invited attendees have declined, you will be prompted to delete the meeting without sending cancellation notices. Otherwise, Outlook will send a cancellation notice to all invitees. That way, no one shows up for a canceled meeting.

If a meeting is canceled that you were planning to attend, you will receive a cancellation message. When the message arrives, click Remove from Calendar in the Reading pane to remove the meeting from your calendar. You can also open the message and click Remove from Calendar on the Ribbon.

Do it!

A-5:   Declining a meeting request

Here's how	Here's why
1 Activate Mail	
2 Select the **YY: Product Planning** message	(If necessary.) The contents of the meeting request appear in the Reading pane.
In the Reading pane, click **Decline**	To decline the meeting request from your partner. You are prompted with three options.
Observe the three options on the menu	You can edit the response; this would give you an opportunity to tell the organizer why you're declining the invitation. You can simply send the response. Or you can decline the meeting without sending a response.
3 Choose **Send the response now**	You have declined the invitation. It is removed from your Inbox.
4 Observe your Inbox	

	After a moment, the decline response from your partner will show up in your Inbox.
5 Select the **Declined XX: Product Planning** message	The message states that your partner has declined the meeting request.
6 Activate the Calendar	
7 View tomorrow's schedule	Because you're the meeting organizer, the meeting is still in your calendar. If you don't want to have the meeting, you'll have to delete it from your calendar.
8 Select the **XX: Product Planning** meeting	
9 Click **Cancel Meeting**	

	To cancel the meeting and delete it from your calendar.
Select **Delete without sending a cancellation**	All invitees have declined, so there's no reason to send a cancellation notice.
Click **OK**	The meeting is removed from your calendar.

Setting up recurring meetings

Explanation

Meetings that occur regularly are known as *recurring meetings*. For example, a quarterly sales meeting is a recurring meeting. You can schedule recurring meetings by setting recurrence options while adding the meeting to the Calendar.

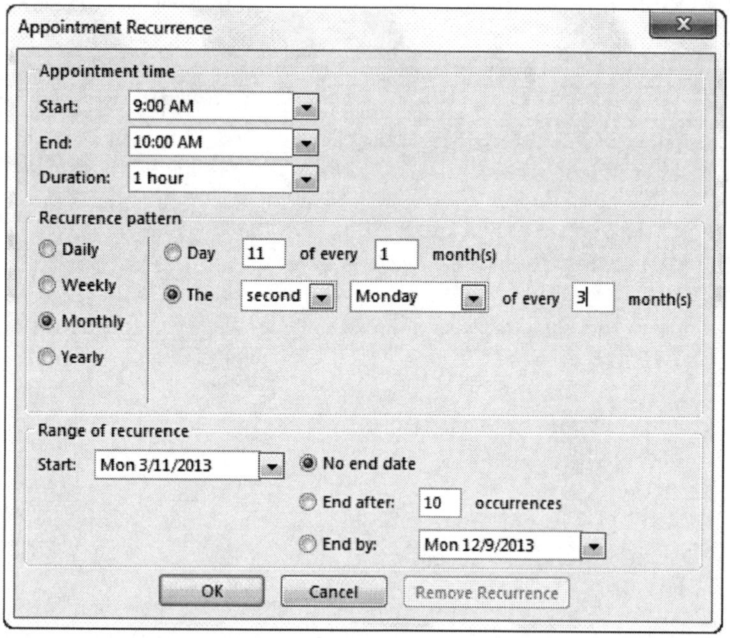

Exhibit 7-3: The Appointment Recurrence dialog box

Required and optional attendees

For any type of meeting request, you can designate attendees as either required or optional. Required attendees must attend; if they cannot meet at the scheduled time, the meeting will have to be rescheduled. The meeting can proceed without optional attendees present.

When creating a meeting request, click the To button rather than typing addresses into the To box. Then select the required attendees and click Required. Select the optional attendees and click Optional. If you enter addresses into the To box, they are considered required attendees.

Do it!

A-6:   Adding a recurring meeting

Here's how	Here's why
1 Switch to Month view	
2 Right-click the second Monday of the month	If that date is already past, select the second Monday of next month.
Choose **New Recurring Meeting**	To open the Appointment Recurrence dialog box. (You can also add a "normal" meeting and click Recurrence on the Ribbon.)
3 Under Appointment time, from the Start list, select **9:00 AM**	
From the Duration list, select **1 hour**	When you specify the duration, the end time is adjusted automatically.
4 Under Recurrence pattern, select **Monthly**	
Set the recurrence pattern to the second Monday of every third month	
⦿ The [second ▾] [Monday ▾] of every [3] month(s)	
5 Click **OK**	To close the Appointment Recurrence dialog box.
Observe the Recurrence information beneath Location	(In the Untitled – Meeting window.) It displays the recurrence settings for the new meeting. You can change these settings by clicking the Recurrence button on the Ribbon.
6 Click **To**	To open the Select Attendees and Resources dialog box.
7 In the Name list, select your partner	You'll make your partner a required attendee.
Click **Required**	
8 In the Name list, select **Instructor**	The Instructor will be invited as an optional attendee.
Click **Optional** and click **OK**	
9 Specify the subject as *YY:* **Quarterly sales meeting**	Where *YY* is your lab station number.
Specify the location as **Conference Room**	In the Location box.

10 Send the meeting request

11 Move your pointer over the
second Monday's meeting

A pop-up with meeting details is shown.

Observe the right edge of the pop-up meeting's box

01: Quarterly sales meeting

Start: 3/11/2013   9:00 AM
End: 3/11/2013   10:00 AM

Organizer: Student01
Location: Conference Room
Reminder: 15 minutes

The circular double-arrow icon indicates a recurring meeting.

Proposing a new time for meetings

Explanation

If a meeting time does not fit your schedule, you can suggest an alternative time instead of declining the meeting. However, the meeting organizer will decide whether to reschedule the meeting or keep it at its originally proposed time. The organizer also controls whether or not attendees can propose a new time.

To propose a new time for the meeting:

1 Preview or open the meeting request message.
2 Click Propose New Time and select either Tentative and Propose New Time or Decline and Propose New Time to open the Propose New Time dialog box, shown in Exhibit 7-4. Here, you can modify the date and time, but you can't change the attendee list.
3 Modify the date and time, or choose AutoPick Next or click the << button to automatically select the next (or previous) available time for all attendees.
4 Click Propose Time to open a new Meeting Response window.
5 Click Send. The meeting organizer receives a New Time Proposed message.

You can propose a new time for a recurring meeting. You'll need to choose whether to propose a new time for a single occurrence or for the entire series when you open the request.

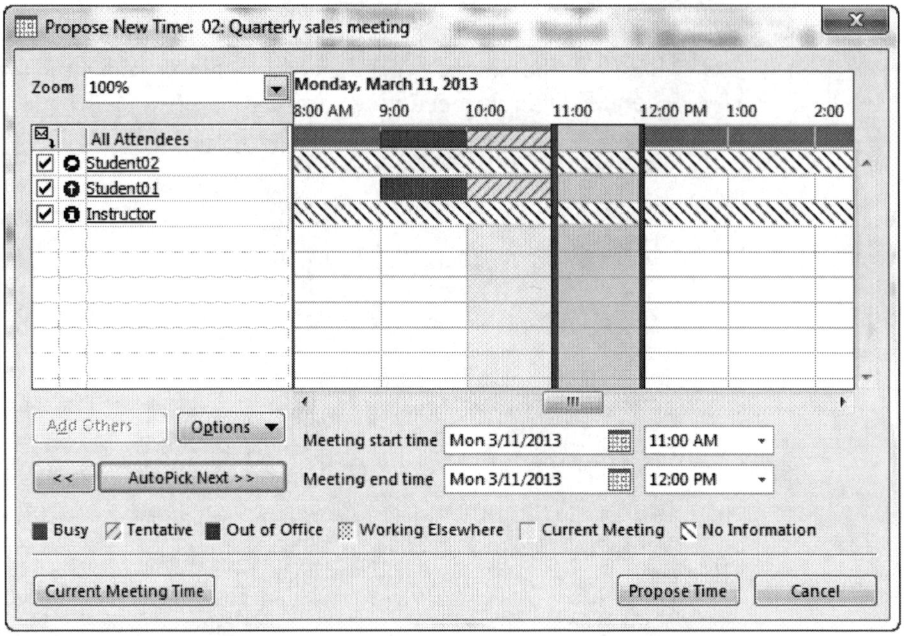

Exhibit 7-4: Proposing a new time for a meeting

Do it!

A-7: Proposing a new time for a meeting

Here's how	Here's why
1 Double-click the **XX: Quarterly sales meeting** invitation	(Where *XX* is your partner's lab number.) Make sure you open the invitation your partner sent to you, not the one you sent to your partner.
Select **Just this one** and click **OK**	You will propose a new time for just this one occurrence in the series.
Observe the buttons on the Ribbon	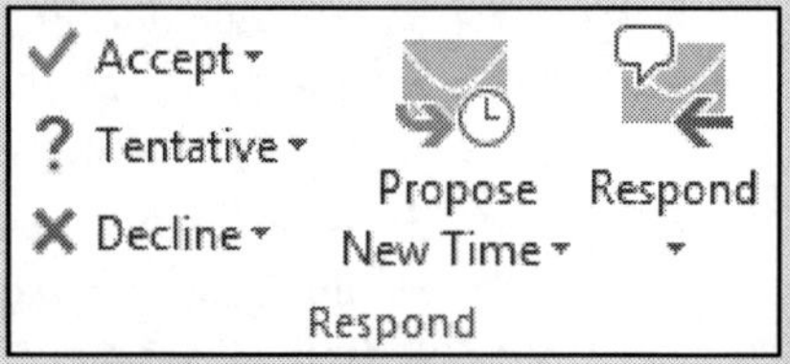 As with the preview, you can use these buttons to respond to the request.
2 With your partner, decide which of you will propose one hour early and which of you will propose one hour later	You and your partner each invited the other to a recurring meeting. You'll reschedule both as you work together in this activity.
3 Click where indicated	 To display the menu.

Select **Tentative and Propose New Time**	To tentatively accept the meeting request but also propose a new time for the meeting. You can also use this menu to decline and propose a new time. (Clicking the top half of the button is the same as opening the menu and choosing Tentative and Propose New Time.)
Observe the time planner	It displays the calendar of all involved invitees and organizers.
4 If you're the partner proposing a later time, click **AutoPick Next**	To select the next available time slot for all attendees and resources.
If you're the partner proposing an earlier time, click **<<**	To the left of the AutoPick Next button.
5 Click **Propose Time**	To open a new Meeting Response window. It displays the meeting's original time and the new time proposed. You could enter a message to the organizer in the message body.
Click **Send**	To send your proposed new meeting time to your partner.
6 Open the **New Time Proposed:** *YY:* **Quarterly Sales Meeting** message	(Don't preview it.) The message states that your partner proposed a new time.
Click **Accept Proposal**	To accept the meeting time suggested by your partner and reschedule the meeting. The Meeting window appears.
Click **Send Update**	To send an update message to the attendees and close the Meeting window.
7 In your Inbox, select the *XX:* **Quarterly Sales Meeting** message	To preview it. You could also open the message.
8 Click **Accept**, and select **Send the Response Now**	On the Ribbon.
9 Activate the Calendar	
Switch to Month view	The meeting has been moved to the newly proposed time.
View the schedule for three months from now	The meeting invitation, which you've not accepted, is listed on the second Monday at its originally scheduled time. You rescheduled only the single occurrence in the series.

Modifying meetings

Explanation

You can modify meetings after scheduling them. When you do so, you will be prompted to resend the meeting request. If attendees accept the changes, the meeting will be rescheduled on everyone's calendar. You can modify both one-time and recurring meetings.

When you modify a recurring meeting, you can modify the entire series or a single occurrence of the meeting. Open the meeting and then select either "Just this one" or "The entire series." Make your changes and click Send Update to send an update to the meeting attendees.

Do it!

A-8: Modifying a meeting

Here's how	Here's why
1 Confirm that you're viewing the calendar three months from now	
2 Double-click **YY: Quarterly sales meeting**	(Where *YY* is your lab number.) You'll modify this meeting. Because it's a recurring meeting, you'll be prompted to choose whether to change just this occurrence or the entire series.
Select **The entire series**	You want to change all occurrences of the meeting.
Click **OK**	
3 Click **Recurrence**	On the Ribbon.
4 If you're partner A, change the start time to **2:00 PM**	The End time is changed for you automatically because Outlook preserves the duration originally set for the meeting.
If you're partner B, change the start time to **3:00 PM**	
5 Click **OK**	A dialog box warns you that any exceptions associated with the recurring appointment will be canceled.
Click **OK**	To set all instances of the recurring appointment, including this month's, to the new time.
6 Click **Send Update**	To send an update to the attendees.

Topic B: Managing meetings

This topic covers the following Microsoft Office Specialist exam objectives for Outlook 2013.

#	Objective
3.2	**Create Appointments, Meetings, and Events**
3.2.9	Schedule resources
3.2.10	Utilize Room Finder
3.3	**Organize and Manage Appointments, Meetings, and Events**
3.3.4	Add participants
3.3.7	Share meeting notes

Explanation

When creating meeting requests, you can reserve resources such as meeting rooms, overhead projectors, computers, and so forth. Reserving resources via meeting requests requires an Exchange Server or third-party components. Additionally, the Exchange administrator must create mailboxes for each resource or perform other configuration steps to enable resource scheduling.

To schedule a resource, you add it to the attendees list, just like you invite a person. From the Meeting window, enter the name of the meeting location or click the down arrow to select from a list of previously used locations. You can also click the Rooms button to open the Room Finder, as shown in Exhibit 7-5, and select a location that has been set up through Exchange Server by your administrator.

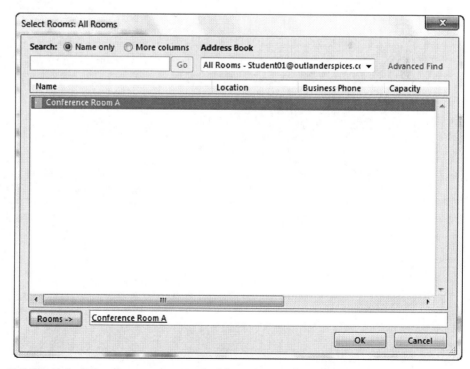

Exhibit 7-5: Selecting a room works like selecting invitees

If you're using the Scheduling Assistant, you can add the resource's calendar to your view to book a free time. If you frequently reserve a resource or you manage a resource, you might want to add its calendar to your Calendar folder.

Do it!

B-1: Reserving resources in a meeting request

Here's how	Here's why
1 With your partner, decide who will be partner A and who will be partner B	Partner A will schedule appointments, events, and meetings at the times printed in the book. Partner B will schedule items at one hour *after* the times printed in the book.
2 Activate the Calendar	
3 Click **New Meeting**	To open a new Meeting window. The InfoBar tells you that invitations have not been sent for the meeting.
4 In the To box, enter your partner's email address	
In the Subject box, enter **XX: Spice Sampling**	Where *XX* is your partner's number.
5 Next to the Location box, click **Rooms**	
6 Select **Conference Room A**	If necessary.
Click **Rooms** and click **OK**	 To... Student02; Conference Room A The conference room is added to the To box.
7 Schedule the meeting to happen on next **Friday** at **1:00 PM**	Partner B, your meeting should start at 2:00 PM.
The meeting will last one hour	
8 Click **Send**	To send the meeting request and close the Meeting window.

Managing responses

Explanation

You need to know how the attendees of a meeting have responded so that you can decide whether to reschedule the meeting or change its venue. For example, if most of the attendees are not available at the proposed time, you'll need to reschedule the meeting or cancel it.

To review the responses of the attendees, open the Meeting window and click the Tracking button, shown in Exhibit 7-6. You can also check the InfoBar to see a summary of the responses, such as Accepted, Declined, or Tentative.

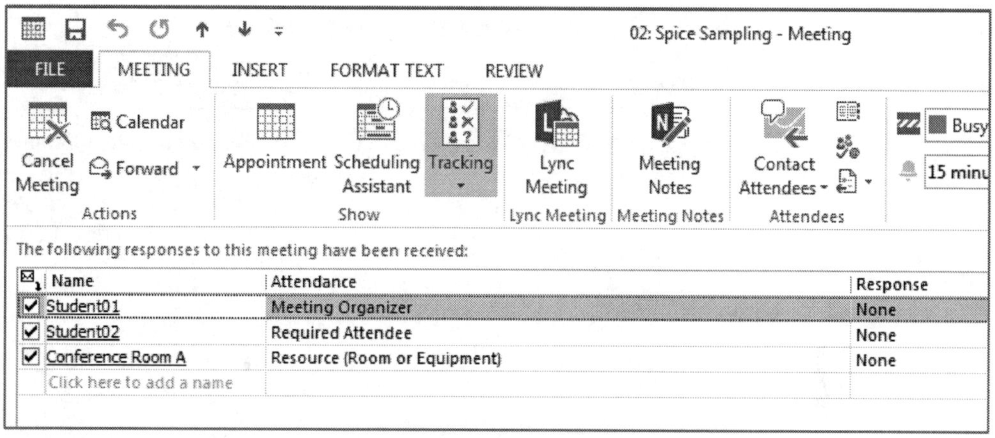

Exhibit 7-6: Meeting responses in the Tracking window

Do it!

B-2:   Reviewing meeting responses

Here's how	Here's why
1 Open the **XX: Spice Sampling** meeting	(Double-click it.) Be sure to select the meeting for which you're the organizer. The InfoBar displays the number of attendees who have accepted, tentatively accepted, and declined your meeting request.
2 Click the top half of the Tracking button	 To display a list of the invitees and their responses.
3 Close the window	

Adding and removing attendees

Explanation

You can add and remove meeting attendees as needed. To do so:

1 Open the meeting.

2 To add or remove attendees, either edit the entries in the To box, or click the To button and use the resulting window.

3 Click Send Update, and choose whether to send the update to just the attendees who were added or removed or to all attendees.

4 Click OK.

Do it!

B-3:   Adding meeting attendees

Here's how	Here's why
1 Open the **XX: Spice Sampling** meeting	Be sure to select the meeting for which you're the organizer. The InfoBar displays the number of attendees who have accepted, tentatively accepted, and declined your meeting request.
2 Click **To**	
Select **Instructor**	
Click **Required**	
Click **OK**	
3 Click **Send Update**	
4 Select **Send updates only to added or deleted attendees**	(If necessary.) You can also opt to send the update to all attendees.
Click **OK**	Only the new attendee will receive the meeting update.

Communicating with attendees

Explanation   Sometimes you need to send additional information to attendees. Perhaps you received a new report that attendees should review before the meeting. You can send a note to attendees by opening the meeting item, clicking Contact Attendees, and choosing New Email to Attendees. Compose your message as usual and click Send.

Do it!   ### B-4: Contacting meeting attendees

Here's how	Here's why
1 Open the *XX*: **Spice Sampling** meeting	Be sure to select the meeting for which you're the organizer. The InfoBar displays the number of attendees who have accepted, tentatively accepted, and declined your meeting request.
2 Click **Contact Attendees**	
Choose **New Email to Attendees**	
3 In the message area, enter **Please bring bottled water or another drink. We'll have many spices to sample.**	
4 Click **Send**	
5 Close the Meeting window	

Canceling meetings

Explanation

To cancel a meeting, open it or preview it. Click Cancel Meeting on the Ribbon. Then click Send Cancellation to send the cancellation notice to all attendees.

If a meeting is canceled that you were planning to attend, you will receive a cancellation message. When the message arrives, click Remove from Calendar in the Reading pane to remove the meeting from your Calendar. You can also open the message and click Remove from Calendar on the Ribbon.

You cannot cancel a meeting without sending a cancellation message. This requirement prevents attendees from showing up for a canceled meeting.

Do it!

B-5: Canceling a meeting

Here's how	Here's why
1 Activate Mail	If necessary.
2 Select the **YY: Spice Sampling** meeting request	You will accept your partner's meeting request so that you can both observe the email messages exchanged when a meeting is canceled.
Click **Accept** and choose **Send the Response Now**	To accept the invitation.
3 Activate the Calendar	
4 Open the **XX: Spice Sampling** meeting	
5 Click **Cancel Meeting**	
Click **Send Cancellation**	
6 Activate Mail	If necessary.
7 Open or preview the **Canceled: XX: Spice Sampling** message	The meeting has been canceled.
Click **Remove from Calendar**	To delete the meeting from your Calendar.
8 Activate the Calendar	
Observe next Friday's schedule	The canceled meeting has been removed.

Unit summary: Meeting requests and responses

Topic A

In this topic, you used the Calendar to **plan a meeting**. You created and sent a **meeting request**, which contains all of the details of a meeting proposal, such as time, date, and subject. You learned how to accept or decline a meeting request. Then, you created a **recurring meeting**. You also proposed a new time for the meeting.

Topic B

In this topic, you learned how to **reserve resources** and **review responses**. You also learned how to update a meeting, add and remove meeting attendees, and send additional information to attendees. Next, you learned how to **cancel** a meeting.

Independent practice activity

In this activity, you'll create and send a meeting request. You'll also open a meeting request, propose a new time, and accept a proposed time change.

1 Create a meeting request with the subject *XX:* **Worldwide sales strategy** for next Tuesday at an hour of your choosing. Send the meeting request to your partner.

2 Open the meeting request that you receive from your partner.

3 Propose a new time, and send the meeting request.

4 Accept the proposal.

5 Review the meeting responses for the meeting you created.

6 Add your Instructor as a meeting attendee.

7 Cancel the meeting.

8 Close Outlook.

Review questions

1 What is a meeting request?

2 What are the four types of meeting attendees?

3 How do you accept a meeting request?

4 True or false? When you decline a meeting request, an entry is added to your calendar so that you can join the meeting later if you change your mind.

5 Do you always have the option of proposing a new date and time if you are invited to a meeting that doesn't work with your schedule?

6 How do you add or remove a meeting attendee?

7 As the meeting organizer, how can you easily see all of the invitees' responses to your meeting request?

8 When you cancel a meeting that you created, can you choose whether Outlook should deliver cancellation notices to the other attendees?

9 True or false? Your Exchange administrator must configure resources, such as rooms and equipment, before you can reserve them via meeting requests.

10 What is the benefit of using the Scheduling Assistant when creating a meeting request?

11 To use Schedule view to see other people's calendars, you must first do what?

Appendix A

Microsoft Office Specialist exam objectives

This appendix provides the following information:

A Microsoft Office Specialist exam objectives for Outlook 2013, with references to corresponding coverage in Outlook 2013 ILT Series courseware.

Topic A: Exam objectives map

Explanation   The following table lists all Microsoft Office Specialist exam objectives for Outlook 2013 and indicates where each objective is covered in conceptual explanations, hands-on activities, or both.

#	Objective	Course level	Conceptual information	Supporting activities
1.0	**Manage the Outlook Environment**			
1.1	**Customize Outlook Settings**			
1.1.1	Include original messages with all reply messages	Basic	Unit 2, Topic C	C-2
1.1.2	Change text formats for all outgoing messages	Advanced	Unit 2, Topic A	A-4
1.1.3	Customize the Navigation Pane	Advanced	Unit 1, Topic D	D-4
1.1.4	Block specific addresses	Basic	Unit 3, Topic C	C-1
1.1.5	Configure views	Basic	Unit 3, Topic B	B-1
1.1.6	Manage multiple accounts	Advanced	Unit 1, Topic B	B-3
1.1.7	Set Outlook options	Advanced	Unit 1, Topic B	B-1, B-2
1.2	**Automate Outlook**			
1.2.1	Change quoted text colors	Advanced	Unit 2, Topic A	A-5
1.2.2	Create and assign signatures	Advanced	Unit 2, Topic B	B-1
1.2.3	Apply Quick Steps	Advanced	Unit 1, Topic C	C-1
1.2.4	Create and manage rules	Advanced	Unit 3, Topic A	A-1, A-2, A-3
1.2.5	Create auto-replies	Advanced	Unit 2, Topic D	D-1
1.3	**Print and Save Information in Outlook**			
1.3.1	Print messages	Basic	Unit 2, Topic E	E-1
1.3.2	Print calendars	Basic	Unit 6, Topic D	D-5
1.3.3	Save message attachments	Basic	Unit 2, Topic D	D-3
1.3.4	Preview attachments	Basic	Unit 2, Topic D	D-3
1.3.5	Print contacts	Basic	Unit 4, Topic A	A-8
1.3.6	Print tasks	Basic	Unit 5, Topic B	B-6
1.3.7	Save messages in alternate formats	Advanced	Unit 3, Topic C	C-5
1.3.8	Create data files	Advanced	Unit 3, Topic B	

#	Objective	Course level	Conceptual information	Supporting activities
1.4	**Search in Outlook**			
1.4.1	Create new search folders	Advanced	Unit 4, Topic B	B-5, B-6
1.4.2	Search for messages	Basic	Unit 3, Topic B	B-3
		Advanced	Unit 4, Topic B	B-1
1.4.3	Search for tasks	Advanced	Unit 4, Topic B	B-3
1.4.4	Search for contacts	Advanced	Unit 4, Topic B	B-3
1.4.5	Search calendars	Advanced	Unit 4, Topic B	B-3
1.4.6	Use advanced find	Advanced	Unit 4, Topic B	B-2
1.4.7	Use Search by Location	Advanced	Unit 4, Topic B	B-1
2.0	**Manage Messages**			
2.1	**Create a Message**			
2.1.1	Create messages	Basic	Unit 2, Topic B	B-1
2.1.2	Forward messages	Basic	Unit 2, Topic C	C-2
2.1.3	Delete messages	Basic	Unit 2, Topic C	C-4
2.1.4	Adding/remove message attachments	Basic	Unit 2, Topic D	D-1
2.1.5	Add cc and bcc to messages	Basic	Unit 2, Topic B	B-1
2.1.6	Add voting options to messages	Advanced	Unit 2, Topic C	C-1
2.1.7	Reply to all	Basic	Unit 2, Topic C	C-1
2.1.8	Reply to sender only	Basic	Unit 2, Topic C	C-1
2.1.9	Prioritize messages	Basic	Unit 3, Topic A	A-1
2.1.10	Mark as private	Basic	Unit 3, Topic A	A-1
2.1.11	Request delivery/read receipt	Basic	Unit 3, Topic A	A-4
2.1.12	Redirect replies	Basic	Unit 3, Topic A	A-3
2.1.13	Delegate access	Advanced	Unit 6, Topic A	A-3
2.2	**Format a Message**			
2.2.1	Format text	Basic	Unit 2, Topic B	B-1, B-3
2.2.2	Insert hyperlinks	Basic	Unit 2, Topic C	C-3
2.2.3	Apply themes and styles	Advanced	Unit 2, Topic A	A-1

#	Objective	Course level	Conceptual information	Supporting activities
2.2	**Format a Message (continued)**			
2.2.4	Insert images	Basic	Unit 2, Topic D	D-2
2.2.5	Add a signature to specific messages	Advanced	Unit 2, Topic B	B-1
2.2.6	Format signatures	Advanced	Unit 2, Topic B	B-1
2.2.7	Create and use Quick Parts	Advanced	Unit 2, Topic A	A-6
2.3	**Organize and Manage Messages**			
2.3.1	Sort messages	Basic	Unit 3, Topic B	B-2
2.3.2	Move messages between folders	Advanced	Unit 4, Topic A	A-1
2.3.3.	Add new local folders	Advanced	Unit 4, Topic A	A-1
2.3.4	Apply categories	Advanced	Unit 4, Topic D	D-1, D-3
2.3.5	Configure junk e-mail settings	Basic	Unit 3, Topic C	C-1
2.3.6	Cleanup messages	Advanced	Unit 3, Topic B	B-2
2.3.7	Mark as read/unread	Basic	Unit 3, Topic A	A-5
2.3.8	Flag messages	Basic	Unit 3, Topic A	A-5
2.3.9	Ignore messages	Advanced	Unit 3, Topic B	B-2
2.3.10	Sort by conversation	Advanced	Unit 3, Topic B	B-1
2.3.11	Set attachment reminder options	Advanced	Unit 2, Topic A	

3.0   Manage Schedules

3.1   Create and Manage Calendars

#	Objective	Course level	Conceptual information	Supporting activities
3.1.1	Adjust viewing details for calendars	Basic	Unit 6, Topic D	D-1
3.1.2	Modify calendar time zones	Basic	Unit 6, Topic D	D-3
3.1.3	Delete calendars	Basic	Unit 7, Topic A	A-3
3.1.4	Demonstrate how to set calendar work times	Basic	Unit 6, Topic D	D-2
3.1.5	Create multiple calendars	Basic	Unit 7, Topic A	A-3
3.1.6	Manage calendar groups	Advanced	Unit 6, Topic A	A-2
3.1.7	Overlay calendars	Basic	Unit 7, Topic A	A-3
3.1.8	Share calendars	Advanced	Unit 6, Topic A	A-1

#	Objective	Course level	Conceptual information	Supporting activities
3.2	**Create Appointments, Meetings and Events**			
3.2.1	Create calendar items	Basic	Unit 6, Topic A	A-1
		Basic	Unit 6, Topic C	C-1
3.2.2	Create recurring calendar items	Basic	Unit 6, Topic A	A-2
		Basic	Unit 6, Topic C	C-2
3.2.3	Cancel calendar items	Basic	Unit 6, Topic B	B-3
3.2.4	Create calendar items from messages	Basic	Unit 6, Topic A	A-3
3.2.5	Set calendar item times	Basic	Unit 6, Topic A	A-1
3.2.6	Categorize calendar items	Advanced	Unit 4, Topic D	D-4
3.2.7	Use the scheduling assistant	Basic	Unit 7, Topic A	A-4
3.2.8	Change availability status	Basic	Unit 6, Topic A	A-1
3.2.9	Schedule resources	Basic	Unit 7, Topic B	B-1
3.2.10	Utilize Room Finder	Basic	Unit 7, Topic B	B-1
3.3	**Organize and Manage Appointments, Meetings, and Events**			
3.3.1	Set calendar item importance	Basic	Unit 6, Topic A	
3.3.2	Forward calendar items	Basic	Unit 6, Topic A	A-1
3.3.3	Configure reminders	Basic	Unit 6, Topic A	A-1
3.3.4	Add participants	Basic	Unit 7, Topic B	B-3
3.3.5	Respond to invitations	Basic	Unit 7, Topic A	A-2
3.3.6	Update calendar items	Basic	Unit 6, Topic B	B-1
3.3.7	Share meeting notes	Basic	Unit 7, Topic B	B-4
3.4	**Create and Manage Notes, Tasks, and Journals**			
3.4.1	Create and manage tasks	Basic	Unit 5, Topic A	A-2
3.4.2	Create and manage notes	Advanced	Unit 5, Topic A	A-1
3.4.3	Attach notes to contacts	Basic	Unit 4, Topic A	A-3
3.4.4	Create journal entries	Advanced	Unit 5, Topic B	B-1
3.4.5	Update task status	Basic	Unit 5, Topic B	B-2

#	Objective	Course level	Conceptual information	Supporting activities
4.0	**Manage Contacts and Groups**			
4.1	**Create and Manage Contacts**			
4.1.1	Create new contacts	Basic	Unit 4, Topic A	A-1
4.1.2	Delete contacts	Basic	Unit 4, Topic A	A-2
4.1.3	Import contacts from external sources	Basic	Unit 4, Topic B	B-2
4.1.4	Edit contact information	Basic	Unit 4, Topic A	A-2
4.1.5	Attach an image to contacts	Basic	Unit 4, Topic A	A-2
4.1.6	Add tags to contacts	Basic	Unit 4, Topic A	
4.1.7	Share contacts	Advanced	Unit 6, Topic A	A-5
4.1.8	Manage multiple address books	Basic	Unit 4, Topic B	B-1
4.2	**Create and Manage Groups**			
4.2.1	Create new contact groups	Basic	Unit 4, Topic C	C-1
4.2.2	Add contacts to existing groups	Basic	Unit 4, Topic C	C-2
4.2.3	Add notes to a group	Basic	Unit 4, Topic C	C-4
4.2.4	Update contacts within groups	Basic	Unit 4, Topic C	C-2
4.2.5	Delete groups	Basic	Unit 4, Topic C	C-5
4.2.6	Delete group members	Basic	Unit 4, Topic C	C-2

Course summary

This summary contains information to help you bring the course to a successful conclusion. Using this information, you will be able to:

A Use the summary text to reinforce what you've learned in class.

B Determine the next course in this series, as well as any other resources that might help you continue to learn about Microsoft Outlook 2013.

Topic A: Course summary

Use the following summary text to reinforce what you've learned in class.

Unit summaries

Unit 1

In this unit, you learned about the common elements of the **Outlook 2013 user interface**, such as the Ribbon, Folder pane, and Reading pane. Then you customized **Outlook Today**.

Unit 2

In this unit, you learned how to compose and send **email messages**. Then you previewed and **opened** the messages to read them. You also forwarded, **replied** to, and deleted messages. Then you learned how to include **attachments** with their messages. Finally, you learned how to **print** messages.

Unit 3

In this unit, you set importance and sensitivity levels for messages and requested delivery and read **receipts**. Then you changed the Inbox **view** and organized the Inbox folder. You also **arranged** and **sorted messages**. Finally, you learned how to manage **junk email**.

Unit 4

In this unit, you learned how to manage **contacts**. You also added, edited, and organized contacts. Then you viewed **address books** and **imported** contact data from Excel. Finally, you created a **contact group**.

Unit 5

In this unit, you learned how to manage **tasks**. You created **one-time** and **recurring** tasks. You also learned how to **assign** tasks and how to accept and decline task requests. Finally, you sent status updates and **tracked** the completion of a task.

Unit 6

In this unit, you learned how to use the **Calendar** to set up one-time and recurring **appointments**. You also learned how to modify, delete, and restore appointments. Then you learned how to add one-time and recurring **events**. Finally, you customized the Calendar views and added **holidays** to the Calendar.

Unit 7

In this unit, you learned how to use the Calendar to send **meeting requests**. You scheduled one-time and recurring meetings. You also learned how to accept and decline meeting requests, as well as **propose new times** for meetings. Then you learned how to **reserve resources**, such as meeting rooms. Finally, you learned how to **update** and **cancel** meetings.

Topic B: Continued learning after class

It is impossible to learn how to use any software effectively in a single day. To get the most out of this class, you should begin using Microsoft Outlook to perform real tasks as soon as possible. We also offer resources for continued learning.

Next courses in this series

This is first course in this series. The next course in this series is:

- *Outlook 2013: Advanced*

Other resources

For more information on this and other topics, go to **www.Crisp360.com**.

Crisp360 is an online community where you can expand your knowledge base, connect with other professionals, and purchase individual training solutions.

Glossary

Address book
A database that contains the names and contact information for people with whom you frequently communicate.

Appointment
A time slot that you reserve on your calendar, such as for a dentist appointment.

Attachment
A file that is transmitted along with an email message so the recipient can see the file in its original format.

Contact
A person with whom you have a business or a personal relationship. You can manage information about each contact, such as the person's name, address, telephone number, email address, Web site address, company name, birthday, and anniversary.

Contact group
A group of email addresses under a single entry, enabling you to send one message to multiple recipients. (Called a "distribution list" in previous versions of Outlook.)

Contacts folder
Also referred to as the *Outlook Address Book*, an address book that is private for each user. You can use your Contacts folder to add email addresses and other information for the people with whom you frequently communicate.

Contents list
The middle pane of the Outlook window; it displays the contents of the selected view.

Date Navigator
A miniature calendar that's used to select a date to be displayed in the Calendar.

Email
An electronic message sent from one computer to another.

Email account
A record that contains the information that identifies a user so that he or she can send and receive email messages. A user can have more than one email account. To access an email account, a user needs a user name and a password.

Email postmarking
A feature that incorporates a digital postmark into messages to help reduce the amount of spam in your Inbox. Messages without postmarks are sent to the Junk Email folder.

Event
An activity that lasts for a period of one or more days and that can be added to the Calendar.

Filtering
The process of customizing your Outlook folders to display only those items that meet certain criteria.

Folder pane
The leftmost pane in the Outlook window. It shows the active pane and contains view-switching buttons.

Global Address List
An Exchange Server address book that contains all of the users, groups, and contact-group email addresses in your organization. All users in an organization have access to the Global Address List. Only the Exchange Server administrators can edit this address book.

Importance
The priority of a message. When you set the Importance level of a message to High, the red exclamation mark that's added tells the recipient that the message needs an immediate response.

Inbox
A folder that contains all of the messages you receive. You can read, create, reply to, forward, and delete messages in this folder.

InfoBar
An area, located at the top of a message in the Reading pane or Message window, that indicates the action taken on the message, along with the date and time.

Instant Search
A feature that appears at the top of the Folder pane and has a text box you can use to enter your search criteria.

Item
Any email message, contact, or task created in Outlook. Items are stored in folders, such as Inbox, Calendar, Contacts, Tasks, and Notes.

Junk email
Unsolicited messages, such as business promotions, advertisements, and messages with adult content. Also called "spam."

Meeting request

An invitation that contains the details of a meeting proposal, such as time, date, and subject. These invitations are sent by email to the invitees.

Message flag

A flag symbol, located to the right of a message in the Message list, identifies the message for further action. When you flag a message, you can specify the action to be taken, the due date, and the time.

Outlook Address Book

An address book that contains a private list of email addresses and is automatically created from your contacts. When you update the contact information, the Outlook Address Book is updated automatically.

Range of recurrence

The period defined by the starting and ending dates of a recurring task or appointment.

Reading pane

A pane in the Outlook window that displays email messages.

Recurrence pattern

The frequency with which a task or appointment occurs. For example, the task or appointment can occur annually, monthly, weekly, or daily.

Recurring appointment

An appointment or meeting that occurs regularly.

Recurring task

A task that needs to be performed on a regular basis.

Search folders

Folders used to locate messages in a specific category or based on a specific condition.

Sensitivity

A message classification that indicates messages containing personal or highly sensitive content. There are four levels of sensitivity: Confidential, Private, Personal, and Normal (default).

SharePoint Services

A technology that enables aggregation, collaboration, and search capabilities for people, teams, and information.

Task

An Outlook item that keeps track of activities that must be completed within a specified period of time. A task has a current status, which can be In Progress, Not Started, Waiting on someone else, Deferred, or Completed.

Task list

A section of the To-Do Bar that displays the tasks for the current date.

Task request

An email message asking the recipient to complete a task.

Tasks folder

The folder that's used to create tasks and monitor their status.

To-Do Bar

A pane in the Outlook window that displays the Date Navigator, upcoming appointments, and tasks.

View

The way data appears in a folder. Examples include Day view and Month view in the Calendar.

Index

M

N

O

P

Q

R

S

T